Dear Donna,
Know that God got you.

love
[signature]
xx

A VERY CIVIL MATTER

Professional Abuse

The ultimate manipulation of the System that is there to protect the Vulnerable and Abused

ELAINE DUFFUS

Copyright 2020 by HFW Publishing Ltd

All rights reserved. Written permission must be secured from the publisher to use or reproduce any part of this book, except for brief quotations in critical reviews or articles.

Publisher: HFW Publishing
Distributed by: HFW Publishing
ISBN: 978-1-8383191-9-9

Author's Explanation

Explaining the He/His/She/Her - capital letters- that may appear in the middle of a sentence.

This is not a grammatical mistake but used deliberately to emphasize this person's character.

For the grammar connoisseur, I do sincerely hope this does not distract from the essence of this book.

Dedication

This book is dedicated to the truly and living God, Yahweh, as without God, I do not know where my children and I would be.

God, I owe you everything because I am who I am all because of God's Mercy and Grace.

To the loving memory of my late mother, Agatha Codner, fondly known as Ms May. She was the best role model of a woman, person, and mother, as with all that she endured; she did it all with the utmost Integrity. I admire that even though my mother was not educated to the highest level; her common sense, wisdom, and kindness of heart was her strength. My mother's own life experiences helped me to overcome the most difficult times in my life; the temporary loss of a child and the dissolving of my marriage.

As difficult as these situations were, my mother reminded me always to maintain composure, integrity and faith. My mother's consistent prayers are what saw me through. She sat at the window, looking out on the world with a faith that never wavered. She prayed. My mother's favourite quote, which I constantly heard as a young child, in troublesome times:

"The cornerstone that the master-builder refuses."
(This is not biblically correct, but this is the way my mum would say it)
1 Peter 2:7 New International Version

My mother would say this and laugh. As a child, I did not understand the meaning, why my mother said this each and every time I went through a problem and wanted to give up. My mother always treated me as her special child; none of the other children were ever treated any less; however, I was the youngest and was given that extra care. I was her princess dressed in gorgeous frilly dresses, very much not liked at the time, by me. However, when I look back, the care my mother took to dress me and do my hair, finishing it off with the cutest ribbon, it was evident how much I was loved. This never changed as I grew into a young woman and eventually becoming a mother myself, her love for me never flickered but increasingly flourished, as I became her young Queen.

As a mother myself, this also became my favourite quote and included in my prayers, especially in times of adversity, particularly with my middle son, whenever he was and is going through difficult times.

My mother passed away in 2014, a victim of Vascular Dementia, always encouraging me regardless and always praying.

My Mum is still, and will always be, my inspiration.

A Daughter's recipe of love for her Mother

Our love is pure
Our love is unconditional
Our love is endless

Add ¼ tiredness
Stir in ¼ patience
Sieve in ¼ of happiness
add a capful of loyalty
add a few drops of success
and sprinkle with a generous portion of gratitude
Gently folding the mixture with care
Place in the oven at a moderate heat
checking at intervals not to overcook
Garnish abundantly with love.
Serve for eternity from a grateful and sincere heart

Elaine Duffus
19/04/2016

My father, Marcus Nehemiah Carr. A loving and kind father, who without fail provided for his family. He was a respected figure of the community, always willing to help others, offering a room – rented or rent-free, to new arrivals from any of the Caribbean Islands. Our home was always full of people he helped. The parties were lively and vivid, with an array of people being offered food and drink. He would always find space.

His plan was that I would be educated in business, and he was the person who purchased my first typewriter. While other children played with their plastic version, he gifted me the real thing; blue, shiny metal. A real typewriter, with black and red typing ribbon, the real McCoy. My new-found passion was born. I wore the most beautiful leather shoes, with my father buying the latest dolls and presenting me with my first black doll. He was my first encounter in a relationship with the opposite sex. We were never hungry or wanted for anything. He worked hard to provide for his family. He was a man who gave gifts, and it did not have to be a special occasion. I believe I take this aspect of giving from my father.

Both my parents taught me many lessons in surviving; emotionally, physically, spiritually, and financially. Lessons that could not be learnt from books alone, and as I grew into a woman, this would not only guide me but help me, to be the daughter, sister, aunty, mother, friend, confidante, trainer, person and a survivor, that I have become today. I am profoundly grateful to God for choosing such wonderful parents to give me too.

To my Princes, Asher, Joshua, and Jonathan, whom I love very much. Each of them have taught me different qualities on the many journeys through Motherhood. Asher has taught me how to be a mother with patience; Joshua has taught me how to be a mother who forgives, and Jonathan - the child I wish I had two of - has taught me how to be a mother who gives unconditional love with no boundaries. All my sons give me a sense of joy, being their Mum.

There have been many that have encouraged me over the years with my writing journey, some positive and some not so positive, not being aware that their behaviour urged me to write. I sincerely thank you either way.

Domestic violence is a systematic pattern of behaviour on the part of the abuser designed to control his partner.

The abuse can be physical, emotional, psychological, financial, or sexual. Anyone forced to alter their behaviour because they are frightened of their partner's reaction is being abused. It can begin at any stage of the relationship. Domestic violence is rarely a one off. Incidents become more frequent and severe over time.

Source: Refuge.org.uk

There are different kinds of abuse that can happen in different contexts. The most prevalent type of domestic violence occurs in relationships. But the definition of domestic violence also covers abuse between family members.

Source: Gov.org.uk

"You plotted evil against me, but God turned it into good, in order to preserve the lives of many people who are alive today because of what happened."

Genesis 50:20 Good News Translation.

Author's Introduction

'Domestic abuse isn't always physical. Coercive control is an act or pattern of acts of assault, threats, humiliation and intimidation or other abuse that is used to harm, punish, or frighten their victim.

Coercive control creates invisible chains and a sense of fear that pervades all elements of a victim's life, and it works to limit their human rights by depriving them of their liberties and reduce their ability for action. experts like Evan Stark liken coercive control to being taken hostage, as he says the victim becomes captive in an unreal world created by the abuser, entrapped in a world of confusion, contradiction and fear." common examples of Coercive behaviour are:

- Isolating you from friends and family
- Depriving you of basic needs such as food
- Monitoring time
- Monitoring you online communication tools or spyware
- Taking control over aspects of your everyday life such as where you can go, who you see, what you can wear and when you can sleep
- Depriving you access to support services, such as medical services
- Repeatedly putting you down, such as saying you worthless
- humiliating, degrading or dehumanizing you
- Controlling finances
- Making threats or intimating you

You can read more in this article written for The Telegraph.
Source : Women's aid until women & children are safe

Two years since the criminalization of coercive control yet perpetrators are yet to feel "the full force of the law" Friday 29th December 2017.

Yet since it was made a criminal offence in December 2015, less than 1% of all domestic abuse-related offences recorded by the police were classified as coercive control, and an even smaller number of these cases resulted in a charge or conviction. As a result, the full force of the law is yet to be felt by those who continue to carry out this appalling crime.

Source : Women's aid
until women & children are safe

I have been asked about the purpose for my writing a book on the roles and responsibilities of professionals in order to highlight the various ways and patterns in which Domestic Abuse may occur, instead of sharing another story around Domestic Abuse.

First, I have to start with saying, I am in no way an expert on the subject of Domestic Abuse and Domestic Violence.

This book is intended to highlight the manipulative and coercive patterns of abusers and show how professionals can play an unrehearsed part, when and how, Domestic Abuse or Domestic Violence occurs. Knowingly or unknowingly, their part can help guard or become a hindrance, if Domestic Abuse or Domestic Violence continues in the same pattern.

Perpetrators are known to find a way around even the most complex and sophisticated systems and orders, and with the assistance of particular professionals, this occurs with ease. Thinking they are above the law, in some cases, it makes it more difficult when the spotlight is turned and shone their way. As even when there is an obvious situation of abuse occurring the perpetrator turns a situation, into an Inspector Poirot, Who did it? With them in the leading role.

"If you are neutral in situations of injustice, you are chosen the side of the oppressor."

Desmond Tutu

A word or look could help that victim be prompted when to talk or act, to the path of self-help, preservation and ultimate survival. Just as equally a word or look can allow a perpetrator to know what they can or cannot do in an act of abuse. The pattern can be broken when the power is limited or taken away – reviewing and possibly reduced contact with the victim at child contact times, asking for the protection of the court - Barring order - Section 91(14), or just plain listening or looking more at the facts can also determine the best course of action for all concerned.

Section 91(14) of the Children's Act 1989 – an order which acts as a hurdle to further applications to court being made in respect of the children in the particular case as it requires a permission hearing each time the parent makes an application.

These orders are considered fairly draconian in nature, but they are not uncommon, and the court will use one if it considers that continued litigation is harming the children or being pursued for the wrong reasons. They can be used as an order of the last resort when there have been repeated and unreasonable applications made by one or both parties.

A court can impose a s91(14) order without being asked to do so, but it usual for one party to apply for it in the face of constant applications made by the other and endless court hearings arising from those applications. The barring order will last for a specified time, often a fixed period of years or until children reach a certain age.

Source: cflp.co.uk –
Cambridge Family Law Practice

The concerns of the children play a large part in the writing of this book and with professionals possibly lacking understanding in reading the situation – following the textbook instead of the signs of abuse; co-parenting playing a huge part and not looking at the best interest of the child's wellbeing. In some cases, the needs of the abusive parent can outweigh the needs of the child. This can and may place the child at extreme risk and danger; turning the other cheek, ignoring, or using the term *'It's a civil matter'*, has seen many victims, Adults and Children, no longer around to tell their story...

PTSD (Post-traumatic stress disorder) and DOMESTIC VIOLENCE

PTSD affects 7.7 million Americans over 18 in a given year. According to the National Institute of Mental Health, it can affect anyone who has experienced a shocking, scary, or dangerous event, which includes women who have been through violence or other trauma.

Source: Zahra Barnes
What is it like to live with PTSD?
After escaping Domestic Violence. Article.

A Messiah Stradivarius

To care for a child, they need to be sheltered
like A Messiah Stradivarius
in the finest leather case

To care for a child, they need to be held in loving protective arms,
always,
like a Messiah Stradivarius
held with 2 loving hands.

To care for a child, they need to be nurtured and loved
like a Messiah Stradivarius protected from the extreme elements of
temperature, dirt, rosin, and oils.

Unlike A Messiah Stradivarius
which is only played a couple of times from its creation,
because of its priceless value,
A Child should never be played.

Elaine Duffus
31/05/2020

Messiah Stradivarius 1737 violin estimates worth US$20 million
Children are priceless

A Very Civil Matter - Elaine Duffus

INDEX

1st	Campaign - Financial	1
2nd	Campaign - Education	21
3rd	Campaign - Police	45
4th	Campaign - Legal	60
5th	Campaign - Football	75
6th	Campaign - The Church	95
7th	Campaign - Refuge Centre	124
8th	Campaign - Mediation - Cafcass	135
9th	Campaign - Children and Family Services	159
10th	Campaign - Medical	166
	Final Campaign	176

Campaign – a series of military operations intended to achieve a goal, confined to a particular area, or involving a specified type of fighting.

"Those who are at war with others are not at peace with themselves."

William Hazlitt

1st Campaign - **Financial**

Financial and Economic Abuse

Refuge, in partnership with The Co-operative bank, launched the powerful 'My money, my life' campaign to shine a spotlight on this often overlooked form of domestic abuse and call for industry-wide agreement to support people who experience financial abuse in their relationships.

Key findings from their study on financial and economic abuse included:
- One in five people in the UK have experienced financial abuse in an intimate relationship.
- 60% of all cases are reported by women
- 78% of women saying their abuse went on over five years compared to 23% of men
- For women, financial abuse rarely happens in isolation – 86% experience other forms of abuse
- A third of financial abuse victims suffer in silence, telling no-one

Source: Refuge.org.uk

Esther had never experienced anything like this in her life. She had come from a loving home with an extremely thoughtful mother. Misleadingly thinking that leaving Him would be the start of her new life with the children. She had this vision of driving off into the sunset or at least down Whitehorse Road, in her sky-blue car, sun beaming down on them. As long as she was away from Him, she didn't care, and by any means necessary, she had to leave Him, for the final time. She was walking away after six years of marriage.

When she met Him, He had explained His debts and how His previous relationship was to blame. This should have been a major red flag, to her, He accepted no responsibility. Well, Esther ignored the red flags but accepted His excuses and even agreed when He blamed others.

It was only after leaving Him that Esther realized that all the bills were in her name, all except the main assets. He had asked for this from the very start always using the same phrase "I feel like I'm walking on eggshells that at any time you will not want me." She always reassured Him that He did not have to worry. He had explained that He could not pay towards anything because He owed 'that money.' He mentioned it like it was a taboo subject, in a lowered voice, always sighing and rolling his eyes.

Esther did not want to put pressure on Him and continued to pay all the bills. She was in a good job and had always managed her money well. She wasn't extravagant and lived within her means. Esther was fiercely independent and always paid her way. She had forgotten with her ex-partner they paid equally for everything. She felt she needed to be understanding to His needs and wanted to help Him, as much as she could. He came with expensive tastes and charm. He had no idea of how to manage bills, as in the past, always returning to his family home after each failed relationship, but she felt it would be different with them. They were committed to making this work.

> During financial abuse, the abuser engages in destructive behaviour that results in the victim experiencing a financial crisis and forming a financial dependency on the abuser. The victim's funds or assets are used solely for the abuser's benefit.
>
> Source: 6 Signs of Financial Abuse
> November 25, 2016 written by Shairesa Ngo
> Cheatsheet.com/money

Everyone thought they were the ideal couple, well-matched in all areas, financially, physically, socially, intellectually, and spiritually, both working in the community sector. He was charming and attentive, especially when in public, but in private, disagreements would turn His way, to make her feel guilty of His financial situation. This would always shame her into grappling with the bills that arrived.

Esther did not mind and saw it as they could build together, and she was prepared to do anything to assist Him, so they could both be on the same level of financial independence.

Esther's parents had taught her well, buying what she could afford, not living off credit. Her frequent holidays abroad were paid for in cash, the clothing and items she bought for her son and herself were paid for in cash. If it was not affordable, then she waited and saved until she could purchase it. Credit and living above her means was not an option. Esther paid her way, and with the only large debt she owed, she had a plan in place to pay this off in due time. Esther was financially secure for her and her son.

The mind games began as soon as they married. The constant wanting her to reassure Him He was good enough and comparing Himself to her ex-partner, who was financially more secure than He was, was used to make her feel guilty.

'But he's got more money than Me why didn't you stay with him?" He used to divert from any of their financial discussions, waiting for her to give the reassuring statements of comfort He yearned for, but if Esther could not find a financial solution, He would sulk in silence, for hours or even days, until she gave in. The silence was a sign of His disapproval, over the years for anything He did not like. Ignoring her with silence became His pattern to dismiss her.

Esther would then have to reassure Him further, and His desires would follow shortly afterwards – installation of Sky, He missed watching His sports - but not in His name, as it was not His home. The circle of behaviour continued whenever He wanted something. There was a moulding occurring to His requests, but Esther just didn't see it, she wanted Him to be comfortable. The mini-series of their life continued, His money was His money, and her money was their money.

There were days He would arrive with an abundance of shopping, all well-orchestrated, usually when one of her family members were visiting, and He would present them with a bottle of wine, to share; He would use her occasional drinking against her later. No one was any the wiser about their financial difficulties, He was always ready to put on the show, as the bread winner and provider, after all, He was the one working and she was self-employed, staying at home to look after the children.

They each had a child, from a previous relationship, and the difficulties from His previous relationship was causing Him distress. He complained his ex-partner wanted more finance, Esther agreed with her. Esther had tried to approach the subject, with Him before, He had said everything was fine, but she knew all was not well.

That Friday evening, He arrived from work, stating it was their weekend to relax and had switched off His mobile, but He was on edge. He was in no way used to having His phone switched off that long, taking it up at intervals just to move it in His hand, almost playing with it. No, He was in no way comfortable it was switched off. Esther attempted to coax Him to switch it back on; after all, He may be needed by His family or His son. He reassured her, she was His sole priority this weekend.

Sunday evening, they had returned from attending church and were seated for their evening meal, the house phone rang. It was His ex-partner demanding money for their son's college shoes. He was furious not for her 'demands' but that she had found a way to contact Him. He raged about how did she get the number? How was He expected to find money at this time, a Sunday evening? Esther felt it for Him and agreed with Him that this was unreasonable behaviour by His ex-partner. Esther had no idea that in years to come she would be the ex that the mobile phone would be switched off too.

The arrival of their first child increased His vigorous demands and spending, where He would return from work with new costly trainers or some new clothing. Each time Esther inquired how He could afford it, considering His debts He was trying to clear, He would then remind her of an item He had bought her, or she had bought herself, even if it were as cheap as £5. He never mentioned the gifts she had bought Him. Esther was under pressure to pay the additional costs, and with the added mouths to feed and His additional expenses, now becoming a strain to her finances. Esther was afraid to ask but had no choice.

Esther decided to make out a list of the household expenses, and they could look through it together and maybe see how He could take on some of the bills, paying it into the rarely used joint account, they had opened only to place their wedding day gift money in.

He listened, and she mistakenly thought this was a sign of a change. After she had spoken, He stood up and walked away. He was going to have a shower, leaving the list on the table. She was stunned. That was that. She just had to carry on. She did not want to argue. He always turned it around, 'Why are you shouting." She had not even raised her voice and would remind her that He was the earner.

The pregnancy of their second child was different and extremely difficult, with her being an older mother, and her feeling unwell most of the time. Esther's frequent visits to the hospital meant she had to be selective with the jobs she took on, being unable to travel far from home.
This was His opportunity to increase His campaign

> It's thought that pregnancy can be a trigger for domestic abuse because abusers take advantage of situations in which the woman is more vulnerable. For some, pregnancy is the perfect time because they think their partner is more reliant on them for financial and other means of support now that they are having a baby.
>
> Source: Babycentre.co.uk

Esther was now hearing it each, and every day, they needed to move.

'I'm walking on eggshells, we need to be equal', was His favourite phrase to make her feel guilty. Esther checked the figures; it could only happen if they both pulled on their resources. She had already cashed in her life savings to help during their first pregnancy to support them financially. This went very quickly due to His ongoing pressure, knowing that her finances were there, she felt obliged to 'help Him get onto the same level as her,' by paying off His outstanding debts. He was now debt-free, just like her. He could now approach His place of work, as they gave out Home-Buyers service for key workers. He reassured her that He would look into it, even waving the paperwork in front of her as proof.

He was ready to move, but Esther could not see a way until He did His part. Regardless, they began looking at larger homes. At each potential home, He found a fault - 4th bedroom was too small, garden not big enough. Esther could see this was not going to happen. They had to move, but there was no way they could afford a huge home, well not the size He wanted. His suggestion was, 'We could if we borrowed a large amount.' She was reluctant; she had never borrowed so much money. He removed all doubts. 'I owe nothing. This will be no problem. Together we can afford to pay it back.

> Less well-known is that banks are not always adequately protecting victims of domestic violence against financial abuse. Whether they do it knowingly or through ignorance, women are being hurt. Sometimes the lack of safeguarding policy hurts women. Other times abusers are laughing at the banks and how easy it is to manipulate them. In my experience, I have found that staff are not properly trained in aspects of financial abuse, so don't take sufficient steps to protect vulnerable victims/survivors of intimate partner violence.
>
> Source: Jean Hatchet.
> The Huffington Post 22/09/2017

They attended the bank, and she hoped that it would not be possible, as she was self-employed. The Advisor at the bank had a solution, to add His name to the lending. She was devastated. She had attended hoping that this was not an option. He was working, and it was the best solution, the Advisor suggested. Esther had lived her life sticking to her financial plans, not going into debt. All assets accumulated were with her first relationship, and these were then to be passed to their son, to care for his additional needs, she had said this to Him.

He sensed her doubts. The Advisor saw no problem with adding His name, emphasizing this again, with a chuckle, 'After all you are married and in love.' Esther felt that twinge of doubt again. He sensed her hesitation, immediately reassured her that nothing would change. Esther was in deep thought, as they both looked at her. The Advisor, sensing the awkwardness, made an excuse to leave, 'I'm going to get some paperwork, while you both think this over." and exited.

As soon as the door of the small room was shut, He turned on her, 'Are you planning to leave me on the street?' The blame cycle began. He had to be reassured; they were solid. She agreed, His guilt trip had worked.

A few months later, as they sat in the solicitor's office, that uncomfortable feeling crept over Esther. His look in her directions, from an earlier appointment, was spotted by the solicitor, and additional documents were drafted. The papers were drawn up to protect her and her son, and the finance was given very soon after.

As soon as the money was released into their joint account. He allocated it for spending. The Mind games began. He would look up to the sky, 'I was at work, and when I looked up and saw a plane, I visualized us being on it.' This happened each time a plane was overhead, followed by a longing sigh. He would also mention His family holidays that He was excluded from and His longing to travel, especially to the US.

Esther had travelled extensively before she had met Him, and Him knowing this information was used to make her feel ashamed of her previous life. Esther booked the holiday. He was so excited, and this then led to Him needing to purchase new clothing for the trip – new trainers to match each outfit, even the handkerchief was used as an accessory, after all, He had not had a holiday since their honeymoon. Again, He reminded her, that His pardona had paid for their honeymoon. Esther soon realized that everything had a price with Him. His initial thoughts were not to provide for His family – If He paid it out, He had to have it back by any means necessary.

Esther was waiting. Understanding the true meaning of His words, 'Walking on eggshells,' she had to choose her time for them to discuss their move and His spending was not helping them to move quicker. He felt the holiday was the start of the 'good life'. Each time she asked how the Home Buyers Scheme application was progressing to add to the now dwindling funds, He replied it was fine, and he was just waiting to hear from them.

They underwent some needed renovations to where they lived. This could add to their funds eventually, but she had not even noticed that He was not placing any finance back to repay this loan. The loan was paying back the loan!!

Her mind was on the pregnancy, which was becoming increasingly difficult.

> Family Violence includes many different types of violence and abuse.
>
> **Emotional and psychological abuse**
>
> This kind of Family violence is when a family members insults, upsets, intimidates, controls, or humiliates another family member. It includes:
>
> - yelling, swearing, and name calling
> - putting someone down in front of other people or in private
> - using words to intimidate or threaten someone
> - doing or saying things to make someone feel confused or less confident
> - stopping someone from spending time with friends or family
> - stopping someone from practising their religion
>
> Source: Family violence: what is it?
> www.raisingchildern.net.au

Her body had never felt like this with her other pregnancies. The added stress of unwelcomed comments and suggestions regarding her being an older mother were not helping.

Esther had to talk, but who could she trust. It was as if God sent her friend, Lorna to call, at that moment, Esther could not hold it. 'They want me to take that test" she tried to pronounce the name, am-no-cen-te-sis. Lorna repeated the word, Amniocentesis and calmly asked, who? Why? and then the question that mattered '" Do you want to take the test?" Esther immediately said No. She had heard negative things about these tests; she couldn't risk it. Lorna breathed in, Esther knew she was holding in her annoyance and was being respectful to His relatives.

'Don't you remember your first pregnancy and how you were being pressured to do that test?' Esther had completely forgotten. Lorna explained they had even met at the McDonalds on Edgeware Road to talk, due to Esther's distress at the pressure. Esther had completely blocked this memory because even as Lorna relayed details of this meeting, she just could not remember it.

Lorna's voice was now showing her annoyance, at the situation, but she was keeping it in check, and she asked again 'Do you want to have the test? Esther was sure 'No'. Lorna's reply was simple "Then don't do it. It's no one's business."

Lorna advised Esther to ignore them and encouraged her to remain calm and relaxed and told her that she was always at the end of the phone to talk anytime and about anything. Esther felt stronger after this phone call. She was being listened to. She could not talk to Him about this as the main pressure came from those family members, who felt she was too old to have another child, those closest to Him, and He was the person relaying the messages back to Her.

The day of the scan came. He was disappointed as He wanted a girl. Esther had wanted a girl too; she was outnumbered with the testosterone in their home. Another female would have been nice, she thought. Yet seeing her baby on the scan, Esther immediately fell in love with him.

The sonographer was concerned; the baby had to be monitored more; he was small compared to their estimated date of delivery. He ignored the sonographer speaking. His disappointment outweighed the major concern for the baby's needs.

Esther looked at Him, and He held her hand. The Sonographer asked, 'Are you both ok with a boy?"

Esther knew what to do. Esther replied she was fine, and he was perfect. She named her baby; he would be her best friend. He insisted He would give him the middle name, using her father's middle name. She knew why their older son was given His father's name as his middle name. She did not mind; her father's name was strong and biblical. Esther did not care; she knew her baby would be just fine.

The baby came 3 weeks early, tiny, beautiful and perfect, the image of her mother, Esther was totally in love with him.

"The fear of being alone can cause a good woman to settle".
www.quotesagram.com

The arrival of their second child saw things become unbelievably difficult. He now felt that the situation was just not fair, and they should move to allow them to have more space. Esther agreed but saw no way this could happen.

Things had deteriorated so much, and she had left Him numerous times, but each time He persuaded her to return. He wanted them to be a family, and so did she. It was the biggest mistake she could have made. The taunts began within a week of each return, with the additional of ridicule and teasing, 'You won't be able to cope without Me, and with two children under 10 and one with additional needs', He laughed at her. Esther believed Him because, on face value, it did seem impossible for her to cope with the children and their additional activities all by herself.

"On average, a woman will leave an abusive relationship seven times before she leaves for good, according to The National Domestic Violence Hotline. Although society might question these statics and how it is possible for survivors to return to their abusers, there are many factors that play into leaving an abusive relationship permanently."
Breakthesilence.org/beat-that-seven-time/static

Esther had left him again, and this time for longer. On realizing, Esther was serious. His 1st campaign began. Everything was stopped. Her requests for finance were ignored, or He would switch off His phone. Now she remembered, all those years ago He would switch off His phone to His ex-partner, stating she was making unreasonable requests for finance. He was doing the same to her, and the feeling of shame overwhelmed Esther. Esther felt she had judged His ex-partner unfairly, by believing His explanation, that His ex-partner, had only wanted Him for His money.

'The pot calling the kettle black", came to mind immediately, now it was her turn to be ignored and be called the money grabber, gold-digger, wanting only His money. Esther should have known better.

He had arrived in their relationship with limited finance and a stack of debts. His ex-partner only asked for money to look after their child. Ignoring the red flags was now to Esther's detriment.

Three days passed, He was still ignoring her calls and texts. She desperately needed milk and nappies for the baby. She scraped the last of the baby milk from the Aptamil tin; she was on her last 3 nappies. The gas meter was now on the emergency, but she refused to ask her mum for help. This was shameful, but more importantly, she blamed herself for having no plan. The 'rainy day' finance was gone. She could not believe she had placed herself and worse still, her children in this situation.

The doorbell rang, and Esther ran to the door, maybe He had come with at least the nappies and milk. She did not care about food; she would find a way for them to eat, but she needed to deal with the baby. She opened the door; it was her mum. Esther was totally shocked; how had she reached here so quickly? They had not too long spoken on the phone. Mum had said that she missed not seeing them. Esther could not tell her she had no money to come down. Mum came in with lots of food, cooked food; the aroma filled the house. Mum asked, 'You cooked?' Esther just shook her head, unable to speak. Mum smiled and made her way to the kitchen to lay everything out. Mum called her, and as Esther entered the kitchen, she noticed the worried look on her Mum's face.

Her Mum searched her face. Esther was getting nervous, and she knew when her mum looked at her, even as a child, she was in trouble.

"What's going on here?" Mum asked, standing with the fridge door open. They both looked at the few food items on the shelves.

Esther just stood feeling every inch the 8-year-old girl who had just received a letter from school for naughty behaviour, and those had happened often.

'The baby doesn't have any milk.' Esther sighed; that was it; she couldn't think of anything else that mattered and looked away. She had learnt as a young girl, not to dare lie to her Mum, she could smell a lie a mile away, and also her mum's favourite phrase sprang to mind –

'Give me a thief any day, but a Liard will end you up in court'.

(Her mum never said liar she always emphasized a 'd' at the end to exaggerate this distasteful word. It was a swear word. As no one likes a liar)

Her Mum returned back to the lounge and took out her purse. '£100 enough?' Esther nodded, she was lost for words, 'and buy my grandchildren some crisp and sweeties.' Her Mum returned back to the kitchen to busy herself in preparing the food for her grandchildren, singing,'How Great Thou Art'.

Esther ran to get ready and ran to the nearest shop. She wondered – 'how did mum know'? God heard her praying hard last night for a miracle.

He arrived the next day with bags of shopping, knocking on the door. She watched Him unload the car and bring the shopping to the front door. She waited for Him to move away from the door and then opened the door, carefully placing every single bag back, onto the pavement. There was a police officer across the road, attending to another home. He shouted out to him, *'Look, she is throwing the shopping on the pavement.'* The officer looked over.

Esther responded, *'We're okay for shopping'*, went back inside shutting the door.

He shouted out *'What am I supposed to do? I bought stuff for the kids.'*

Esther replied, *'Eat it yourself, we're all okay here.'*

Esther thought back to the conversation she had had with her Mum the night before.

'If you stay, I'm here, and if you leave, I'm here.'

Her mum reminded her never to go without food and not to hide anything like this from her again. Having her Mum not judge her was all Esther needed to make her decision, in her own time, no pressure. Esther had always felt loved.

> Domestic violence is the most common form of violence against women. Household surveys in 57 countries were conducted to determine attitudes towards domestic violence. When asked their opinions, on average, half of girls and women aged 15-49 responded that a husband or partner is justified in beating his wife under certain circumstances.
>
> Source: Attitudes towards domestic violence - Unicef.org

The court date arrived. Esther was stunned by the allegations of Domestic Violence and a list of abuse, dating back from the beginning of their marriage. All financial contributions were established - Payments to the children and other costs. She only wanted a minimum contribution of £200 for the children and agreed to stop CSA involvement. He had told her He was struggling financially. She felt sorry for Him. The car was a birthday gift. He told the court. Esther's solicitor interjected into the hearing that her client had paid the deposit for her 'birthday gift' and made monthly payments each and every month, for the past 2 years. The judge granted that she kept her car, as long as she kept up the payments, and He had to pay towards the household bills. Esther was just grateful she was no longer with Him. The nightmare was over, Esther didn't care about the money she would find a way to cope without Him.

Esther loaded the car that morning, her mother's health was failing, and she had to check on her as much as possible. The last to be loaded into the car were the children. Esther returned to the car to be greeted with a large yellow label stuck to the driver's side and the yellow car clamp. She was stunned and tried to call Him. The text message came back, "Stop harassing me at work."

She returned back inside. They knocked at the door. They had come to take the car back and needed the keys and logbook. She handed over what she could find, panicking, the keys. She tried to explain, *'But I was going to pay today.'* They were surprisingly understanding but were there to do their job. They allowed her to take out her and the children's stuff from the car, suggesting she contact the finance company. She rang the finance company immediately. They explained. *'Even if you paid now, he does not want to be connected with the finance of the car.'* He had shown a total disregard to her previous car and drove it with such aggression she had to get a new car; the only way was by finance and in His name. Esther had made the mistake of letting Him know that her previous partner had purchased that car on behalf of her. She had saved hard to purchase that car, working extra shifts and paid cash for her beloved burgundy Golf.

He showed His resentment when He drove it – changing gears with such force she could hear the clutch shudder through the car, in protest, when He was behind the wheel.

The only child to understand the implication of not having a car began to cry, asking questions. How were they going to get to school? Football? See his Nana? Take Nana to the hospital? Esther simply answered, 'on the bus'. He bawled even more.

He would not answer her calls or texts, continuing to reply she was harassing him at work. Esther was puzzled; they had not argued or disagreed in anyway. Esther had heard of her friend's ex-partners taking back the car but never dreamed it would happen to her. He knew she needed the car. She loaded the buggy. She and the 3 children would get the bus; she had to see her Mum.

Arriving at her Mum, Esther was quiet, and she did not want her Mum to worry, *"They took the car."* Her son started crying to his Nana.

Her Mum looked at her, inquisitively. Esther explained she was going to pay for the car today, but He had them take the car away today. Her Mum went to her bed, not saying a word, and arrived back with her bank book. She handed it to Esther. Esther refused to take it. Her Mum words were calm and firm, *"Leave enough to bury me. My grandchildren will not go on the bus."*

Esther took the bank book, remembering her mother's words, 'leave enough to bury me.' She got her purple Mercedes, that just about allowed them to complete most of their journeys, kicking out black smoke every time she accelerated.

In the still of the night and with each episode, was Esther's time to go her place of prayer and to cry, the children could only see their mum smiling and happy. Music was her love, and her lifeline – the beautiful tones of Tamela Mann filled the room – God Provides. Esther was lost in her own thoughts, and the words lifted her out of her own situation. She had received the help she needed.

Years later, Esther was clearing out her stuff, and she opened one of her hat boxes, Curled in the box was a letter written by her son, the son that knew the implication of not having a car.

> *One day it was a bad time for Mum*
> *this is what happened. Dad took my Mum's car.*
> <u>*Let's Pray*</u>
> *Our father you are the best let the sunshine upon us*
> *in Jesus name Amen*

Esther asked her son when and why did he write this letter? He said when the car was taken, he was sad, and he couldn't talk about it at the time, so he wrote to God. Esther knew he had experienced a significant degree of pain witnessing this event, having their only means of transport removed so suddenly.

> CMS support for domestic abuse or violence. If you have experienced domestic violence or abuse, the Child Maintenance Service (CMS) can help you get money; the other parent is supposed to pay you. You don't need any contact with the other parent to get help from the CMS
>
> Source: indirect.gov.uk

Esther called the CMS (Formerly known CSA) after waiting 4 months and being fed up with borrowing from family and friends. His excuse was He couldn't pay, as He was paying for 4 loans on the go, it was her fault for the break-up of their marriage, her alleged anger, her alleged drinking, her not letting go of the past, even post-natal depression, everything and anything was raised as her fault. As far as He was concerned, it was her fault and blame, for everything that had not gone right in their relationship.

The telephone operator was fine until Esther asked how long this would take to contact Him.

"Why don't you just sort this out between you two. It would save so much time."

Esther said, *'Thank you. I will wait.'* Totally defeated. She had no money and now no choice but to ask her mother again.

Over the years Esther had to contact them, several times, to query when payments were late or reduced. Each time she had to wait an hour or longer, only to hear the same phrase, *'Why don't you sort this out between you'*, but this time she was prepared. *'If I could, I would.' I tried that, and my children ended up with nothing from Him.'* With each phone call, she became stronger, and she mentally prepared herself to react calmly.

It was a year now, and CMS no longer removed His maintenance payment from His wages, He was to be given a chance to make payments directly into an account Esther had chosen. She informed

CMS that one of the children's accounts would be best, as after all, it was their finances. Her niece's words rang out each time she went to take out His contribution - *'He's only contributing. In no way did it cover the needs of the children.'* Dinner monies, school uniform, new trainers, clothing, food, not forgetting the unexpected accidents.

Esther was totally against it, but they informed her it was non-negotiable. This would mean He would have the power to put the finance in within 11 days. Esther did not check the amount to the exact penny, but she knew there was a figure she was expected to receive for both children. Payments were regular and arrived no later than the first of each month. He was consistent.

Suddenly, random emails arrived, not with their usual title about the children; this was titled deduction.

"As you have decided to be the dishonest Christian re the month of May and June payment £14.28 has been deducted from this month's money."

She did not understand. The second email was even more confusing.

"We had not made any attempts to advise re the month of May and June payments but instead be the usual money grabber." Sent from His iPhone.

Esther was totally puzzled now. That day she was due to receive His 'contribution', and she noticed it was £14.28 less. She made some calls to seek advice

---

It is important that both parents tell CMS about any changes in their circumstances. Changes could affect how much child maintenance you pay or receive. You should report any changes within seven days.

Source: NIdirect.gov.uk

Esther called CMS to check what He was talking about; she knew that asking Him would be pointless, with Him either replying with an email that was not related to her query or just plainly ignoring her email, so she decided to go to the source. They informed her, He was correct to make the deduction as He had made an overpayment the previous months.

Esther stared at the letter in front of her. He paid His amount and CMS informed her of another amount. Esther was totally confused with the paperwork and the figures. She hadn't look at the letter or working out in-depth in the last 7 years, until today. The call operator went on to explain, and Esther got total clarity, and the very rose-tinted glasses were definitely removed. There were arrears He owed the children in back payments, and He had asked to pay this at the lowest figure, £5 a month. The call operator explained He had explained His circumstances and they have to listen to His reasons. Esther figured He would end up paying the children £5.00, even when they were adults!! Esther thanked the call operator for his help and hung up. Esther was learning that not every battle was worth fighting, and this one was not worth fighting.

His campaign was being established. She could imagine Him showing all who would listen *'She called CMS on Me for £14.28. She loves money.'*

He wouldn't explain, that at any given opportunity He would inform the children that He gave their 'money' to Esther and they were to ask for anything, regardless of the costs, as the money was there or that unless Esther gave them 'snack' money, at contact times, He wouldn't feed them. Esther's niece's shock revelation was that He had revealed to the last penny the amount He had paid over to the children. Esther could not even remember what she spent last week on them; the spending never stopped.

> Financial abuse is still abuse. When it is all an abuser has left it becomes a powerful weapon that he sharpens with sadistic glee.
>
> Source: Jean Hatchet
> The Huffington Post 22/09/2017

Five years after divorce, a woman's income is 9% lower on average compared with the average divorced man whose income is 25% higher.

#LETSMAKEITRAIN
Rainchq

2nd Campaign - **Education**

Educational Abuse

'Schools are the single biggest opportunity we have to eradicate domestic violence....... '

'Children who see or hear domestic abuse will be suffering from emotional and psychological harm, which is a child protection issue. Schools need to integrate awareness about domestic abuse in order to safeguard the children effectively.'

Source: Safeguarding: Domestic violence written by Dr Julie Leoni published 05 May 2016.

They had decided that their oldest son could not attend a state school. His difficulty with his speech was evident and placing him in a state school environment they both felt would not benefit his needs or give him the help and attention he required. Independent education was not their first choice purely due to the costs; however, Esther had always wanted her children to have the best.

Esther spoke to several people on a suitable school, and with His agreement, they both signed the consent form without hesitation, and the decision was made.

The first day of school is usually nervous and distressing for some children but not their son. Dressed in the grey tones of his uniform, looking very much like 'Just William', dressed in his grey wool perk cap, pure wool embroidered blazer and grey shorts with his crisp pale blue shirt, he was all smiles as he bounced out of the car. Esther was nervous; she was not sure if they would be able to understand him; his words at aged 4, were slurred and sounded muffled. He saw nothing wrong; they were paying for it; they would look after him. He remarked flippantly. She ignored Him. This would be the beginning of His disparaging comments regarding their son's paid education.

The day seemed to drag, Esther anxiously waiting for the end of the school day. They waited outside in the grounds for their son to come out of school, he loved it, smiling and hugging them both. This school suited their son's temperament, which was kind, softly spoken, caring and would nurture him through the education system. Esther was not doing it for prestige, she wanted her son to have the best start, and if that meant she had nothing, eating beans on toast, she was fine with that.

Initially, He was accepting, enjoying driving into the grounds and His voice changed to nearly high pitched, she almost expected Him to say, 'oh gosh', in His most aristocratic tone, just for effect. On realizing He would have to forgo His luxuries – holidays, expensive items, new trainers, there came a flood of resentment towards this expense. Her mother stepped in when He pulled away with the costs; she wanted to support her grandchild. He was her youngest grandchild, and she saw no reason why she should not help him have the best education.

'I know lots of people educated without jobs', was His standard remark. Any sign of her leaving him or disagreeing, He would remove even the slight help with the school fees. She had asked Him several times to help with the school fees. He would then change the subject back to it was her fault for the end of their marriage, each and every time. He would cite His family felt it was a waste of time.

Her mother strongly objected to her grandchild moving school, especially as he was doing so well, with his speech improving steadily, and she contributed where necessary.

He would use His absence, from the family, as an opportunity to 'treat' Himself with gifts He felt He needed, trainers, clothing, upgrade his phone, gym membership, whatever He fancied. Since leaving Him, He finally made it clear He was refusing to pay anything towards the school fees or anything else. He did not have it and could not afford it.

> Every foster child for whom there is a planned placement of three months or more or who remains in placement for longer than three months must have a savings account set up by their foster carer....'
> 'The money saved in that account is for the future needs of the child or young person, when they move into independence or leave care to return to their birth family.'
>
> Source: Policy and Guidance Payments of Fees And allowances to Foster Carers for year 2014-15

Esther remembered some funding connected to her son, with the words being spoken, *'If you ever needed anything for the baby, then come and ask for it.'* Esther had never had the kind of relationship with His family to ask for anything and definitely not money. His court witness statements outlined that due to the pressure that Esther had placed on Him to give finance to the children, these witnesses felt compelled to give Him money for the children's needs. Esther could not deny He had received finance from these witnesses; however, she could confirm this was not received by her or the children.

Esther reluctantly asked Him to approach His family for help with the school fees. At first, He agreed to ask, but each time the discussion was raised He would reply *'I forgot' 'Its wasn't the right time'*. But when He realized, She was ending the marriage; His blunt response was *'Why don't you go ask them yourself. They did not say that to me. They said that to you.'* He laughed, knowing Esther would never approach them for help. That laugh never with a positive end.

> In an anonymous survey whose results were published in 2006, psychologist Stuart Twemlow noted that 45% of the teachers surveyed admitted to having bullied a student. The survey defined teacher bullying as "…a teacher who uses his/her power to punish, manipulate or disparage a student beyond what would be a reasonable disciplinary procedure." Teachers may bully students for several reasons. One being lacking training in proper discipline techniques.
>
> Examples of Bullying
> - Belittling or intimidating a student
> - Singling out one student for punishment or ridicule
> - Humiliating or shaming students in front of classmates
> - Yelling at a student or group of students
> - Using racial or religious slurs or other forms of belittling a student based on gender, race, religion, sexual orientation
> - Sarcastic comments or jokes about a student
> - Public criticism of a child's work
> - Consistently assigning poor grades to one student on objective assignments or projects.
>
> Source: Signs Your Child's Teacher is a Bully
> By Kris Bales Updated June 08, 2020.
> www.thoughtco.com

The outstanding amount on the school fees was now increasing, and Esther had no option but to find another school and pull their son out of this school. Esther was being treated differently and mentioned this to a friend, Sonia. Her reply reassured Esther she was not imagining it – *'If you feel it. It's true.'*

Their continual avoiding eye-contact, the usual pleasantries of 'Good Morning', from some of the teachers, was missing, but she thought only she was seeing and experiencing it.

Esther arrived to collect James from school. The teacher stood and beckoned Esther to approach, using her forefinger, she had a matter she needed to discuss. James' head was down. Her son had been given some water and had not said please. Esther looked at her waiting for more of this situation to come. The teacher went on to say he was not polite in class, not listening. Esther looked at James, not to reprimand him but in surprise. Esther asked James whether he had anything to say. He shook his head. Esther knew this was not how he was, always a polite and kind child, with exceptional manners. She agreed to talk to James, and they left. They walked to the car in silence. As they sat in the car, James turned to her 'Am I in trouble?'

Esther looked at her son feeling so very sorry for him, but if he were wrong, then she would not be able to support if he had disrespected an adult. 'Tell me what happened.' She asked.

James explained that he was given some water and had replied thank you, but the other children was making so much noise, and the teacher had not heard him. His head was still down as he spoke to Esther. When the teacher asked him to say thank you, he said *'Ms I did say thank you,'* then she became angry and started to shout at me. *'Mummy, I did say thank you'*, he replied apologetically. Esther knew he was telling the truth and reassured him not to worry. On the drive home James asked, *'Mum why did she say, "and you can tell your Mum and Dad"? she knows I don't see my Dad. They don't like me Mummy.'*

Esther knew she was unable to ignore this last statement from her son; she had to address this and other issues. She had noticed the deterioration in his spelling grades, he wasn't receiving homework at weekends, and the final straw came when he cried at receiving a low grade in a Maths test, one of his strongest subjects. The Maths teacher's response was *'I am very disappointed in him.'*

Esther turned to James that evening, and she made a promise to him. If anyone told him that they were going to call her or his dad, he should not ever be afraid, but he must always make sure he had not done anything wrong or lied. Esther reassured her son that she would always support him. Esther also reminded her son to hold his head up high regardless. That evening their 'feeling book' was introduced. Esther was now seeing proof but was still unsure around the incidents or attitudes towards her and now her son but knew it had now changed.

At the beginning of her son starting this school, Esther had felt there was mutual professional respect between the teaching staff and herself over the years; this had certainly changed, especially since she had left Him. Their son was a talented sports person and had represented the school in many of their sports activities, in and out of school.

Esther was reluctant to approach the school to discuss her concerns, but her son's remark left her no choice. She was now paying an arranged amount, as she had advised the school of the situation with her estranged husband. They were very understanding and even informed her 'this was not the first time that couples had separated, and the first thing fathers do is to terminate the school fees.' Esther was shocked and embarrassed, but mainly for their son. She really thought He had the best interests of their son in mind.

Esther had no option but to approach the school of her ongoing concerns regarding her son's deterioration in his academic achievement. The Head Teacher listened attentively to Esther's concerns – low spelling grades, not receiving homework when he missed a day from school to represent the school - Esther finished and waited.

The Head Teacher measured her chosen words carefully, sipping her diet coke throw a straw, then it came as she reminded Esther that the school fees were overdue. Esther sat there stunned, the penny finally dropping. She was being told not to complain. Esther asked to meet with the Bursary, who was married to the Head Teacher. Esther thanked the Head Teacher and asked how she could give notice for her son to leave. The Head Teacher would not hear of it, and she was sure they could come to an arrangement. Esther clicked into gear; they needed her son to represent the school at events; however, the thought of a scholarship was not possible that year and had never been offered in previous years. Esther thanked her for her time and left. Esther made some phone calls and discovered that scholarships were to be offered to families in need, however at this school they were being offered to families where no such financial assistance was necessary; a Solicitor's family, who played a large role in the school activities, for example.

Esther decided to walk home and saw a car pull up beside her. She stopped, 'Esther' they knew her name. She turned and saw it was one of the parents, Anita, from her son's school, she offered her a lift.

Anita was a cheerful Guyanese woman, who always gave kind and encouraging words to other parents. She explained she had been calling Esther for the longest time. Esther just couldn't hold in her feelings and began to recount the meeting with the Head Teacher. Anita listened until Esther had finished.

'Your children will thrive wherever and whatever school they go because of the mum that you are.' Esther was speechless; she had not expected such kind words.

Anita went on to say, *'You're a good Mum, and you will do the best for your children.'*

As Esther left Anita's car, she thanked her for her encouraging words. Esther raced home and began looking for different schools and collected all the documents she needed for the meeting with the Bursar.

The Bursar was a friendly cheerful gentleman who listened to Esther's concerns and confirmed her estranged husband had signed all documents, and he would be calling Him in immediately. The account was split equally, and another arrangement was agreed.

He tried everything not to pay the school fees, but it was no use, the contract was signed. He agreed He wanted their son to attend but just did not want to pay the fees. He arrived at all events along with His family members in attendance, walking around the grounds of the school, meeting and greeting all He could.

Their son with lots of tears left that Easter holidays, moving to another school, in year 5. The school he had attended since the age of 5.

> Whether a child is making the transition from primary to secondary school or starting a new school because the family has moved to a different area, she or he is likely to need extra support from parents and other family members at first.
>
> Source: Changing schools.
> www.familylives.org.uk.

The move to a new school Esther saw as a new beginning for both boys. His younger brother was already attending the new independent school, for the past year, and Esther had a good relationship with all teachers. The arrival of her middle son would see a great change and bring her premonitions to the surface.

The letter arrived for the court date. He had changed her name, adding her maiden name to His surname. She found this very strange. They had discussed this before their marriage and Esther had decided on using just His name. She was not to know the consequences of His action. He was unhappy that James had been moved from his school without His permission and wanted to know what school he was attending, no mention of the refusing to pay the school fees. After a year of showing no interest in the school their younger son was attending, He now wanted to know this information.

Esther attended court and without hesitation, informed the court of both of their sons' school. He asked that He not be liable for any school fees. Esther agreed.

His access to the new school brought immediate noticeable changes, from being greeted with a smile, now returning to her previous experience – to teachers avoiding eye contact, no smile, very brief short greetings and, in some occasions, moving away from Esther at an alarming pace.

Esther remembered an incident with His older son from a previous relationship. He was angry, and she sat as she watched Him pace up and down their lounge. She couldn't understand it. He was in a rage because He was not invited to His son's school for any events – parents evening, school social events. What had made Him annoyed was that Esther and her ex-partner attended their son's events. Esther had explained that this had been decided when their relationship ended that they would show a united union for their son's wellbeing. Esther stressed this would have to continue even after their marriage. He had agreed, but it was as if the penny had dropped. He was not invited to any events for His son.

The penny now dropped for Esther. His ex-partner had had good reason for not allowing Him to attend school events.

> Studies show that living with domestic violence can cause physical and emotional harm to children and young people in the following ways: ongoing anxiety and depression, emotional distress, eating and sleeping disturbances.
>
> Source: Effects on children facs.nsw.gov
> The effects of domestic violence | Family & Community Services
> 24 Sep 2019

The planning for secondary school for their oldest son was the next step, and Esther was not looking forward to this at all.

He wanted to have contact with His sons, even when informed that the effects of this were taking its toll on their oldest son. He ignored this, calling the night before the written test. Their son was reluctant to speak to Him, but Esther insisted he spoke to His father. Their son had a good chance of attending a particularly good school, with a scholarship this could be affordable. This resulted in their son becoming extremely stressed and physically unwell; Esther felt he should not attend at all. James wanted to do the test; this was the school he had wanted to attend for the longest time and did not want to miss this chance. Esther agreed but in the pit of her stomach knew he was not ready. Attending court, Cafcass and Mediation, plus not eating or sleeping well, did not place him in the best position to sit this or in fact any test.

The test did not go well, and their son was profoundly upset, blaming himself for not remembering how to answer the questions. Esther reassured him; he had done the best he could on the day. The invitation to their Sports Scholarship Day was totally unexpected. James attended and told her he felt that he had done very well in the football test and had played with older boys.

Esther had not informed His father; she just could not take the chance of Him sabotaging this opportunity for their son. She sat in her car late Monday evening, waiting for her son to finish his weekly tutorial. She had to make the financial sacrifice to give him any extra help. The telephone rang, and the name of the secondary school appeared. Esther answered the phone. She listened and knew her son was not attending this school. How was she going to tell him? She thanked them and hung up the phone. She cried, not for herself, but for her son.

He had visited and informed them of their situation, and they did not wish any difficulties to occur at their school.

James' reaction was expected, Esther reassured him that they would find a good state school, using the excuse that this was more affordable for her. Her son agreed. She further encouraged him he would do well in any school. Esther felt destroyed, but this was not seen by her son. Esther did not feel the need to tell her son that his father had visited the school.

> Am I legally obligated to force visits if my child does not want to go?
> The legal answer may be "Yes" even though the ethical answer could be "no", in some situations.
>
> Source: www.nolo.com

James had made the decision not to have contact with his father. Esther had tried to persuade him to go, buying expensive and unaffordable football boots, playing to his caring nature to attend to look after his younger brother. He refused. He looked up the Rights of Children online and planned that at his next contact visit he would not attend. He would remain in school, placing himself into the school's afterschool club, refusing to leave. The school had no choice but to ask his father to leave. Esther was called. Their son ran out of school and jumped in the car, his face a picture of happiness. It reminded her of his first day at school. She had not noticed, until then, he had not smiled lately.

The courts agreed their son was not to be made to attend contact with his father, with the provision he could attend in the future, if he changed his mind. Esther was to make him available.

> Often in these higher conflict families, where court is the only option, the children are much less likely to adjust, and often the damage has already been inflicted whilst the parents were still together. Some typical high conflict parent behaviour can be;
>
> - Asking children to carry hostile messages to the other parent
> - Arguing openly in front of the children
> - Asking children intrusive or accusatory questions about the other parent
> - Creating a need for the children to hide positive feelings for the other parent
> - Putting down the other parent in the presence of the children.
>
> Source: How Court Proceeding can Damage Children of Separating Parents February 23, 2017, written by Frances Place

Esther found an old picture and showed it to James; she personally felt he looked cute. Her son's reaction shocked her, *'I was depressed Mum. All those visits and courts dates.'* Esther knew he was low, but the being depressed shocked her, having no idea he was feeling that low. He smiled at her, *'Don't worry, Mum, I'm good now.'*

Their younger son's wish was to continue to see his father and Esther saw no issue and even welcomed the break.

Court was daunting, with every court date, Esther felt uneasy. The building felt stuffy, and she could smell the damp in the ancient bricks. The allegations at each court date were more extreme. Boys will be boys and their younger son, was no different, forever coming home with scratches and cuts and, on face value, nothing really to be noted by her. She never even asked the school for their usual slips to note injuries.

> Unfortunately, accusations like child abuse happen quite often in high-conflict custody battles, tempers can escalate quickly, and both parties are bound to feel the strain in some situations, one parent may be tempted to believe that accusing the other parent of child abuse will increase his or her chances of winning child custody. But it's a flawed strategy.
>
> Source: Very Well Mind article written by Jennifer Wolf updated 2020

Esther arrived in court to read the latest court statement. '_____ has sustained a mark to his face.' Esther read this several times. This did not feel comfortable; the way it was written was as though it was an unexplained cut. But he had fallen over at school, why was this being included in a court statement? Was she being accused of injuring their son? No way!

> ### Recording accidents and injuries at schools
> ### What should be reported?
>
> Accidents and injuries should be reported. No matter how trivial you consider an injury to be, you must ensure that it is reported and recorded within school at the time it happens. Injuries which seem trivial at the time can have longer term serious consequences, and the existence of a record can, as mentioned above, subsequently be very important in securing compensation.
>
> Source: Neu.org.uk/advice/accidents-and injuries -school

Esther was totally unprepared for this; she had to seek advice on how to deal with it. She attended the school and asked for a copy of the accident report and was told there was no report on file. Esther spoke to her son's class teacher and asked whether they could write an accident form on her son's accident.

The class teacher was unsure if they could as they couldn't recall the date as this should have been noted at the time and, more surprisingly, queried if this had even occurred at school. Esther asked to speak to the teaching assistant who had been on duty and had informed her of the accident. Fortunately, Esther had collected her younger son that day and knew the date as well as the person who had administered first aid to her son. They agreed to write it up and then gave her a copy. Esther also requested that in future any accident that her son was involved in, no matter how small, that this needed to be noted on his file and she be given a note to reflect this also.

This was now her standard request even when her younger son moved to his new school.

Esther knew this was the time to move their younger son. With the ongoing embarrassment at contact with his brother and father, he was very much up for the move to a new school, especially with his older brother moving to secondary school. Esther was now finding her finances very much stretched, with the continual court case. She found a school and informed Him of the details of the new school by email.

A new school move was an excellent prime ground for Him to make changes in His favour – changing contact dates and times, giving out previous or outdated court orders. However, this time Esther tried to be more prepared, by informing the new school of updated court orders and the necessary contact arrangements before He had contact with them.

Esther was thankful, their younger son settled into the new school very well, making new friends immediately.

The first time He made a non-appearance to collect their son from weekend school, Esther thought it was a mistake. Maybe He had confused the weekends, all excuses she gave Him. After being called a few more times, she realised she would always have to be on standby. When Friday came, and she saw 5.30 pm, she could relax into her weekend as she knew He had collected their son from school.
Esther received the call at 5.50 pm to collect her younger son, she drove crying. She just could not understand why she had not been contacted sooner.

She had done all she could, and with the present order, she was not allowed to attend the school when it was His contact weekend. He had not sent an email to say He was not having their son that weekend. Esther arrived at the school and looked at her son and burst into tears. How could He just not turn up? The teacher present shielded her by standing in front of her, so her son could not see her cry.

They left the school building, and, in the car, Esther asked why he was so upset and suggested he could have just asked the teacher or one of the TAs to call her.

'I told them mummy to call, and they wouldn't listen. I told them "my mum does not know I am here. It's my dad's weekend. Mummy, I cried so much, and they wouldn't listen.' He then told Esther the name of the Teaching

Assistant. Esther knew her younger son was the most articulate of all her children and was not one to give incorrect information. He was her little 'parrot'; he would say exactly how things happened. She did not doubt him.

Esther checked him as soon as they arrived home, a peck flow test, she could hear his chest wheezing slightly. Esther knew he had become so upset it had affected his chest. He was asthmatic, and his distress at not being collected could have been fatal.

Esther felt the best way was to meet with the Safeguarding Officer, especially after the latest incident.

Initially, Esther thought the meeting seemed to go well with the Safeguarding Officer reviewing the present child arrangement order, on the whiteboard in the class. The Safeguarding Officer, after the review, decided, in the interest of the child, to refer this matter to their local Social Services. Her involvement and decisions from this meeting were to change, as things usually do once, He is believed. The letter she received from the school Safeguarding Officer was to inform Esther that the school policy was not to become involved in disputes or separations with parents. The court order was clear with contact.

- The child won't feel heard or seen
- The child's feelings and reality will not be acknowledged
- The child will be treated like an accessory to the parent rather than a person
- The child will be more valued for what they usually do for the parent than for who they are as a person
- The child will be taught that how they look is more important than how they feel
- The child will be taught to keep secrets to protect the parent and the family
- The child will learn not to trust others
- The child will feel used and manipulated

   Source: The real Effect of Narcissistic Parenting on Children
   Posted Feb 19, 2018
   www.psychologytoday.com

Esther's reply letter explained she was unable to attend on His contact times and had no way of knowing if He was not collecting their son for His weekend contact. The school was adamant, Esther and their father were to make the necessary arrangements as to who would collect their son. The school was to remain neutral.

The next 18 months was to be the most stressful time Esther and her younger son had ever experienced. Esther had to change her plans to protect their son from feeling abandoned. She arranged and paid for an appropriate adult, to collect her son, if at any time her son was not collected. Esther made a promise to her son; he would never be left at school again. This was not only protecting their son but covering herself, she could not attend the school, as this would breach the order. A change of Leadership saw a complete turnaround in the school policy. Although the person remained the same, the title had now changed from Safeguarding Officer role to Family Worker/Designated Safeguarding Lead.

Esther decided the wellbeing of her son was paramount, and she needed to approach the school again but now to go above the Family Worker and go to the new Head teacher.

The needs of the child were paramount, each and every time she heard this quoted; she felt a churning in her stomach. It was stated but never implemented.

> Narcissists and narcissistic people are notorious for picking fights at family events, behaving badly on special occasions like birthdays, holidays and anniversaries and acting like seasonal wrecking balls.
>
> Source: flyingmonkeysdenied.com

The appropriate person arrived to collect their son from school, but He had arrived earlier and taken their son. This was not His contact weekend; however the Family Worker agreed He could take their son, not seeing it necessary to check the schedule of contact, Esther had sent through at the beginning of each term.

Esther telephoned the Head Teacher who recognised the error. He agreed to call Him and explain their error. The Head Teacher called Esther back. He would not be returning their son until the next day, Saturday at 7pm. The Head Teacher apologised profusely. Esther should have been prepared. It was a significant date, Mother's Day weekend. The order was clear – their son would spend time with each parent, on their weekend contact time; however, specific parents celebrations would be upheld. It was His weekend; however, it was Mother's day weekend, so Esther was to have their son that weekend. What better way but to attempt to ruin that weekend, by taking their son.

Esther waited in all day Saturday. Their son returned at 7 pm. He was totally confused. *'Mummy, I said it wasn't my Dad's weekend, but she was too busy talking to my dad. I don't like the things she said about you to dad.'*

Esther listened. The manipulation was confirmed. The Head Teacher wrote a letter of apology for the 'error on their part.' but refused to acknowledge that a member of staff had deliberately colluded with Him.

Esther was numb, feeling she had unknowingly enlisted in a Civil War.

This was not to be the last of the disruptions on contact on significant dates. He collected their son when a birthday was planned with her oldest son. There was nothing she could do but just await the return of her younger son and rearrange celebrations. Esther was now prepared at each birthday or special event for a second date of celebration to occur, the boys needed to have happy memories, even if they were a day or two late.

Happy Childhood memories May boost physical and mental health in later life. ….Studies have shown that memories of positive relationships likely serve many functions: They instil us with a sense of gratitude, make us feel good and give us hope for current and future relationships.

Source: Newsweek.com 5 Nov 2018

He tried to change contact, especially before half term and Summer holidays; however, Esther would now send a reminder of the schedule, before these planned breaks, this was for consistency for their son. She planned everything around these dates, and any last-minute changes would mean their son would have no memories with them as a family. He called and notified the Family Worker the dates had to be changed, due to his work rota. She checked the schedule and informed Him it was not his weekend.

He would then email Esther to say he was changing the contact weekend due to his work rota, not realising Esther was now not afraid, and she knew she did not have to change contact dates or times. But more importantly, her son was becoming older and wanted to stay at home more. His email arrived. He was collecting their son even though it was not His weekend contact.

Her past choices were either to go early, removing their son from school or to allow Him to take their son. Esther knew this could not continue.

Previously, Esther had met solely with the Head Teacher, this time she requested a meeting with Head Teacher and Family Worker. Esther confirmed with them that this was not His weekend and suitable arrangements to cause the least disruption to the school and their son were formulated. Esther emailed Him again, reminding Him it was her weekend for contact.

She arrived at her usual time to collect their son and noticed His car parked outside the school. He started to make notes. She was used to this as His way to take her back to court, so it could be noted as Esther breaching the court order regardless of the fact that it was her weekend contact. She foolishly thought as He had spotted her, He would make His notes and then leave. She was completely mistaken. He walked into the playground. Her heart was pumping; she had not had close contact with Him in the last 8 years other than when they were in court. He looked at her, turned and left, speaking on His phone. He met the Family Worker, as He was leaving 'Mum is here so I will leave.'

A Very Civil Matter - Elaine Duffus

His plan had not worked. He had felt His email sent the day before contact would deter Esther from attending. In the past, the fear of returning to court would cause Esther to surrender to His demands; but not now, she was stronger and had no intention after all these years to be intimidated by His emails, and the fear of returning back to court was no longer there.

Esther stood in her own right, making her stance. These were just mini 'battles', and she was no longer prepared to retreat from them.

> Over the years, It was assumed that children who experienced abuse, don't talk about it. However, recent research shows that children do disclose. The big question we must ask ourselves as practitioners is whether we are listening accurately?
>
> Source: Child Abuse: the 'art' of listening? written by Sam Preston | Published: 09 June 2017

Esther thought a turning point had arrived, and the school was placing their son's needs as paramount. She was again mistaken.

Her younger son, seeing her new strength, now began to self-advocate; he did not want to attend contact with his father. He had arrived to collect their son, and their son had asked to speak to his teacher, who in turn spoke to the Family Worker. The Family Worker made the decision that their son was to attend weekend contact as per court order. Esther had experienced this before, holding back the tears, she dared not say anything, fearing she would be accused of 'coaching' her younger son, she hoped it was a one-off incident. Each and every time leading up to the contact weekend, her son asked not to go, speaking to his teacher, Family worker and even the Head Teacher. The blanket statements from The Family Worker and Head Teacher were, 'it's his dad's weekend', or 'you'll have a nice time.' Her son was devastated. Esther knew returning to court was not financially possible; she had only just recovered from the last court proceedings. She had paid off the legal fees but was now working through the debts she had had to ignore to pay them.

Esther requested his school file. Nothing was noted. The file was basic, admissions application and a few correspondences. The constant communication between Esther and the school was missing. Her son's concerns for Esther's safety were not noted. The Head Teacher had informed her, during parent's evening, that her son had requested to meet him and told him his feared His father would kill her. Esther knew of this but had told her son not to tell anyone, as they wouldn't believe him anyway. *'Of course, He won't do that not with the job He does'* The Head Teacher dismissed her son's concerns with a flippancy that astounded Esther.

Esther formally requested a copy of her son's school file. She received the basic information; name, address, a few sheets of notes regarding everyday incidents. No notes of her son's continual refusal to attend contact or her son's fear that his father may kill her. She made another formal request for further details missing from the school file. The Head Teacher informed Esther that the information she had already was the only information on her son's file. No notes of the disruptive parent contact, ongoing working with the school and no notes of her son's comments or concerns or even her ongoing meetings with school professionals. Absolutely no information of substance.

The Head Teacher asked Esther to come in for a meeting to discuss this further. Esther declined. She was learning meetings with professionals were just another way of nothing being produced in a situation and was an exercise purely to be seen to be doing something. A paperless exercise, 'talk is cheap', sprung to Esther's mind, and this was getting emotionally expensive.

Esther asked again for the documents on her son's file, and the Head Teacher telephoned her to advise that due to Data Protection and His name being on particular documents, they could not give her those documents. The Head Teacher confirmed to her that if this matter were to return to court, the school would make the necessary contribution, once asked to do so. Esther informed the Head Teacher she couldn't afford to return to court.

Esther asked why staff had neglected to document her son's refusal to attend visits with his father. The Head Teacher was amazed that this had not happened. Esther explained no one but the court could change contact times however the school had a duty of care to log when a child makes a request, even if the school was not able to assist, everything should be documented for his safety. The Head Teacher excused himself abruptly from the telephone conversation; he had another meeting to attend and was already late.

> Black women have become victims of negative stereotyping in mainstream American Culture. Such stereotypes include the myth of the angry Black woman that characterises these women as aggressive, ill-tempered, illogical, overbearing, hostile and ignorant without provocation.
>
> Source: The Angry Black Woman: Article was written by Wendy Ashley 2014, 29,(1) 27.34

Esther knew from this brief conversation that she was now being seen as a 'difficult pushy parent', a view she was all too familiar with. She had decided she may not have the finance to help her son, but she would not remain quiet. Her driving force was to get her son the necessary help, and this school was now ignoring the legal requirements for safeguarding her child.

> School counsellors typically do the following.
> - Help students understand and overcome social, behavioural problems through individual and group counselling.
> - Provide individual and small group counselling based on student's needs.
> - Work with the student to develop skills such as organization, time management, and effective study habits
> - Help students set realistic and career goals
> - Develop strategies with teachers, administrators, and parents to help students succeed
> - Teach classes on topics such as bullying, drug abuse, and planning for college or careers after graduation
> - Identify and report possible cases of neglect or abuse
> - Refer students and parents to resources outside the school for additional support.
>
> Source: www.sokanu.com

Esther had asked for their son to be enrolled with the school counsellor as with the increased contact with his father, there was a noticeable change in his behaviour; he was becoming more withdrawn and had been getting involved in a few altercations at school. Once Esther raised concerns over the lack of notes on her son's file, she felt that this service too was just an exercise by the school to be seen to help. Her son was now complaining that he did not feel listened to; he was becoming disillusioned with the professionals involved in his life. Esther had heard this before, with his older brother. *'I tell the counsellor everything and no one's listening.'*

Esther just listened, feeling helpless; to move this forward would mean returning to court. She reassured her son, but even that felt hopeless, she could not afford the practical help he needed.

His constant breaches to the order seemed an attempt to return it back to court, but why? Esther just could not see His motives; after all, she had surrendered to His requests.

Safeguarding and child protection in schools.

Schools play an essential role in protecting children from abuse. They have regular contact with children and young people, so they are in a strong position to identify signs of abuse and neglect.

Your school can safeguard children by.

- Creating safe environments for children and young people through robust safeguarding practices
- Ensuring that adults who work in the school, including volunteers, don't pose a risk to children
- Making sure staff are trained, know how to respond to concerns and keep up to date with policy and practice
- Teaching children and young people about staying safe
- Maintaining an environment where children feel confident to approach any member of staff if they have a worry or problem

Source: www.learning.nspcc.org.uk/safeguarding-child-protection-school

> Operation Encompass is a partnership between police and schools, One of the principles is that all incidents of Domestic abuse are shared with the school, not just those where an offence can be identified.
>
> Source: Operationencompass.org

During the lockdown, their youngest son refused to attend contact, both meeting Him and sending WhatsApp messages, to say he no longer wished to attend contact.

When the schools returned, Esther knew He would go to collect their son as usual. Esther sent though the schedule of contact before the September start to school term. He did not attend His first allocated contact weekend, but she knew He was coming.

No email arrived to inform her that He was picking up their son. Esther sat at home frantic, had their son gone to weekend contact or had he been taken by a stranger? Esther sat waiting.

James arrived from school, and Esther informed him she would go for a walk, maybe his brother had decided to go to the local park.

He always arrived home at a particular time, and he would text or call to say he had left school.

Esther walked not sure where to walk, as she did not want to miss her son if he went another route.

Esther telephoned James, to ask if his brother had arrived home, as they spoke, there was knock at the door.

Esther was reluctant to give their youngest son a front door key, as she had done with his older brother, as she did not want Him to have access to their home.

Their youngest son was home. Esther was awash with relief and quickly walked back home.

Their youngest son had gone with his father, he did not want the embarrassment in front of his school friends, if there was a disturbance, but when He had entered the local chemist, their son had used this opportunity to run away from Him and run home.

Their son had run away from Him. Esther knew he did not want to go but to run away was still an uneasy feeling to comprehend.

The school had no option but to listen to their son's request not to attend contact.

2nd October 2020, He arrived at the school to collect their son. The Head Teacher calls Esther; their youngest son does not wish to attend contact. Esther knew she could not make their youngest son attend, but she knew this meant more trouble for her.

But she was not afraid.

**Having courage
does not mean
that we are unafraid
Having courage
and showing courage
mean we face our fears
We are able to say
"I have fallen
but I will get up."**

Maya Angelou

3rd Campaign - **Police**

Nowhere to turn:
Women say Domestic abuse by police officers goes unpunished.

> Beyond the number of allegations, the figures suggest reports of alleged abuse by police are treated differently. Just 3.9% in England and Wales ended in a conviction, compared with 6.2% among the general population. Less than a quarter of reports resulted in any sort of professional discipline. Greater Manchester Police, one of the country's biggest forces, secured just one conviction out of 79 reports over the three-year period.
>
> Source: The Bureau of Investigative Journalism
> 01.05.2019 written by Alexander Heal

Esther had just returned from church. It was an absolutely beautiful day. The weekend had gone well with them attending a friend's wedding the day before. The private number appeared on her phone; she listened to the message. The police had been looking for her and the children over the weekend. She asked why. It transpired there had been a report for the children's safety; the police operator replied rudely to Esther's questions.

Esther panicked, stepping out onto her balcony, she called her niece, who advised her to remain calm and just to answer their questions. Esther informed the boys that the police were coming to see if they were okay, and the oldest son began to cry, followed by the youngest son. He cried because his older brother was crying. Esther tried to remove this doubt as best she could, but even, she was apprehensive with this visit.

Two police officers arrived, one officer, going into their bedroom, with the bedroom door ajar, to talk to the boys. The other police officer spoke with Esther in the lounge. The officer explained their father was concerned because one of their sons did not attend a football match. Esther calmly replied, *'That was strange, He and the club were aware their son would not be attending games for a while.'* Esther then explained she had to take the summer off due to the loss of her mother earlier that year.

She had not grieved her mother's death that year and needed to rest. From the look on the officer's face, she knew he was now uncomfortable and sincerely sorry, without hesitation, he called the other officer to leave. The other officer came into the living room, began giving Esther huge praise about the boys, *'Your children are great. Your oldest son has beautiful writing. He even writes better than me.'* Esther forced a smile at the compliments, seeing them to the door. She could not get over the fact that He had called the police to check the children, and they had been looking for them.

This was to be the first of many weekends that He would attempt to ruin, but she wasn't to know this.

Non-molestation order

A non-molestation order is a special injunction that aims to prevent a partner or former partner from harming you or your children. By harm, we mean actual or the threat of physical violence, any form of harassment or intimidation, as well as psychological abuse.

Source: www.qualitysolictors.com

His knowledge and power of this system showed in His calculated plans from years before. They had already separated, and most, if not all, discussions were regarding arranging contact with the children. Esther was served with a Non-molestation order. He made no mention that for every text she sent He sent at least two, but it was not about who sent it, it was about laying the grounds for a court case of abuse to go in His favour.

She repeatedly read the order absolutely stunned. How could His reasons for bringing this matter to court be as was stated?

Cancelling gas/electricity on Him, threatening and abusive call /texts, damaged His car and clothing, all 8/10 incidents listed with 3 Cad numbers.

Esther had no knowledge of how this would impact ongoing contact with authorities, especially the police.

He had laid the 'the elephant in the room' that only He knew was there, and Esther was to find, hopefully not too late.

Jerry Karlin, chairman of Families Need Fathers, said the result of the government's "well-intended but ill-conceived changes" to the family courts system was a 30% increase in non-molestation orders (NMOs) to 25,000 a year.

There had also been a 20% rise in private family court applications over the last two years, he added.

"These (NMOs) are used in allegations of abuse, and they don't have to be true to obtain access to legal aid."

The Charity stresses that they are useful in genuine cases of abuse but were concerned that the way they were administrated left them open to exploitation. For example:

- They are often granted in the absence of the person being accused of abuse (the respondent) and without accusations of domestic abuse.
- The making of an order that also enables the complainant to draw thousands of pounds in legal aid which can also be used in any subsequent family law cases
- The respondent would not automatically be entitled to legal aid, however, and often had to represent themselves
- The level of evidence required is fairly low and can relate to claims about verbal abuse, unwanted text messages or emails.
- This can lead not only to the parent being physically separated from their children but to being ostracised by the agencies involved.

Source: Extractions from article BBC News Thousands misusing abuse orders to get legal aid says parenting charity. 03 July 2018.

Esther had reported Him several times - sitting outside her home for over an hour and on one occasion He was exercising outside for nearly 4 hours and she had to ask a friend to come and collect her and the boys, leaving in another car.

His continual breaching of the Child Arrangement Order was relentless, with each report she did being met with, 'it's a civil matter.' She now believed Him 'They give Me heads up whatever you try to do to Me.' This stuck in her mind; she could even imagine Him smiling with confidence. No action was ever taken. She could not understand why she was never believed.

She reported Him for Harassment, and He was called to the local police station. No action. She gave pictures of physical abuse - No action.

She showed them abusive emails - No action. Each and every report was dismissed as a civil matter, as it was all around contact with the children or her allegedly trying to cause Him to lose his job. Esther wanted to keep His job, as least she knew that for 12 hours 5 days a week He was occupied.

Esther decided this was not working and that she would go direct to His manager. She called His place of work, leaving a message with one of His colleagues, for His manager to call her back, giving her name. She did not feel it was fair to give details of her complaint to His work colleague.

Esther arrived for another court date and read His statement, noting at the bottom of His statement where His work colleague had informed Him, she had called, and she was going to be charged with a Harassment warning. Esther felt totally at a loss, having a sinking feeling in the pit of her stomach, that He had set up more damaging allegations and for this one, Esther needed to be more than prepared, as her liberty could be at risk.

> The police appear to be able to issue harassment warnings if a complaint is made, without needing to investigate. The subject of the warning cannot contest it. And unlike a caution, it can be imposed even if the subject contests the allegations and puts up a defence. The warning cannot be appealed.
>
> Source The Guardian – Does a harassment warning amount to a penalty without a fair hearing article by Emma Norton 09/09/2010

Esther was calm in the interview room, answering all questions. He was regurgitating evidence again, but He had presented it differently to the police.

No, she had not punched out his teeth.
No, she had not scratched him.
No, she had not bitten him.
No, she had not wanted him to lose his job.

With each question she answered, the duty police appointed solicitors nodded in her direction. Esther had only just met her on that day, when she arrived at Walworth Police Station, with them having only a 15-minute discussion. The duty appointed solicitor just had time to show Esther His allegations and evidence before being called into the interview room. Esther asked if she could ask a question. The police officer replied this was not a discussion and He asked the questions. Esther continued to answer the police officer's questions. Esther was checking the time, and He asked if she had somewhere, sarcastically, she had to be. *'Yes, I have to pick up my younger son from school.'*

This statement seemed to soften His approach to her, and He informed her, she wouldn't be there much longer.

Interview completed the police officer asked her if she wanted to ask any questions.

Esther seized her moment and took out the evidence He had given in at court. There was one photograph, presented at court, that she allegedly had bitten Him and the same photograph now showing that she had allegedly scratched Him. Esther said she was confused about what He was alleging her to have done. The police officer said she would be informed of the outcome, avoiding her question. Another paper exercise but in no way to benefit her. He was definitely going to use this, but how? Esther was not sure.

Once outside, Esther breathed in the fresh air, and the sunlight warmed her face. The room she was interviewed in had no windows so she couldn't tell how long she had been in there and coming out to the sunshine was a relief. She had had a feeling on entering this building that she would not come out after that interview. The duty solicitor was impressed and said so. Esther looked at her and said. *'I'm telling the truth.'* Esther thanked her and went to collect her son from school.

Esther waited for the reply. After months of 'investigations' the letter arrived, she scanned the page, 'No further action.'

> Police officers and staff across the UK were reported for alleged domestic abuse almost 700 times in the three years up to April 2018, according to Freedom of Information responses – more than four times a week on average. The real figure is likely to be higher as data was only provided by 37 of the UK's 48 police forces (including specialist forces)
>
> Source: The Bureau of Investigative Journalism

Esther sat at home waiting, she had spent 5 years waiting for the return of their youngest son from contact, missing events due to waiting but it was a new contact order, and her other children needed to be dropped off or collected. He had made His feelings clear about her first son she'd had from a previous relationship, saying that he was not His concern, but His own son was now being affected. That did not seem to matter either.

Esther had now waited for 3 hours. The police were called. He had made a report earlier to say He would be returning their son later that day. He was unsure what time He was due to return their son, and they were out enjoying themselves. That was the excuse given, and the police officer she spoke to made her feel she should be grateful that He was spending time with their son, and she was being unreasonable with the return times. That old familiar feeling of 'You should be grateful He's having His child', washed over her again.

The police officers were unable to tell her much due to Data Protection, and they could not even tell her the time He was planning to return their son. Yes, His pattern had changed. He was becoming more defiant in breaching the Child Arrangement order. A few minutes late was now turning into a few hours late. The only option was to return back to court, but she had no money for this.

Domestic abuse affects women from all ethnic groups, and there is no evidence to suggest that women from some ethnic or cultural communities are more at risk than others.

Whatever their experiences, women from Black, Asian or minority ethnic communities are likely to face additional barriers to receiving the help that they need.

If you are a Black, Asian or minority ethnic woman trying to escape from domestic abuse, your experiences may be compounded by racism, which is pervasive in the UK. You may be unwilling to seek help from statutory agencies (such as the police, social services, or housing authorities) because you are afraid of a racist response.

Source: Full article Women's Aid. Until women & children are safe
The Survivor's Handbook Women from BME communities.
Women from Black, Asian, and Ethnic minority communities
www.womensaid.org

'Can't you just sort it out?'

Oh Yes, Esther wished she had a pound for each time she had heard this, she could pay off her legal costs. Esther hung up the phone and waited until she could wait no longer. There was a definite shift in His pattern. He had now notified her by email – It was pointless her contacting the police as He had contacted them earlier. Leaving home with a heavy heart, she waited, only for their youngest son not to return on time again.

She drove, barely focusing on the road and with urgency, she had to drop off and pick up and get home. Esther returned home, driving into the poorly lit car park behind her home. As she moved her car to position it to park, she slammed on the brakes as their youngest son ran in front of her car, crying, he was frightened.

She opened the door quickly, and he jumped in. They both began to cry in the car as she grabbed her phone from the cup holder, dialling the police, screaming that He was in the car park and could they come over as quickly as possible.

He was on His phone, looking at her calmly.

The police arrived after 10 minutes looking at the court order, agreeing the return time was correct; however, this is a civil matter, and this matter would have to return back to court

She showed the police officers His email, deliberately returning their son late. They agreed, however, she would have to return this matter back to court. One officer plainly spelt it out, *'This order has no teeth'*. Esther looked puzzled. The officer explained, *'This order did not contain a statement of power of arrest.'* Esther suddenly felt like a great big boulder had been dropped on her from an almighty height; this paper was not worth anything. She always thought that to breach an order was straight to court or even prison. She corrected herself. He always made her feel this was solely her punishment if she did not abide by the order. He knew its power and control.

Esther thanked them as they left. She checked her emails. He had sent several emails, one to inform her He was going to return their son, half an hour before He arrived to drop off. Once He arrived, He emailed her again, and as she was not at home, He emailed again threatening to drop their son at Brixton police station for her to collect him. She got it now, that is why their youngest son was frightened. This was not the first time their son had been taken to the police to report her for not being at home. However, He never informed the police that He had again failed to return our son on time.

'Mummy, Dad told the police you were not at home.'

Esther had seen Him on the phone when she had arrived home. She gave her son something to eat. Her son had informed her his dad didn't cook, relying on his elderly parent to feed him or He gave him cereal or Hardo bread. Once her son was in bed, Esther called the police.

Yes, they confirmed that CAD numbers were raised by Him, against her. Esther gave several other dates, He had not returned their son on time, and each time He had now changed CAD numbers to raising CHS number. She was confused. The operator explained they were the same thing.

> When a crime is reported, a CAD number is allocated to it, and someone should be sent to investigate it. Computer Aided Dispatch is a method of filling reports used not only by the police but also by other organisations such as taxi firms.
>
> Source: WWW.Gov.uk/your-rights-after-crime

> CHS number Criminal History System The Crown now has direct access when a case is in FOS or SOS to CHS and, where the Crown has a 'S'(CHS) number, it can request the criminal history record attached to the 'S'(CHS) number.
>
> Accordingly, prior to submitting witness statements, the Police will carry out a CHS check for all civilian witness marked for citing. In most cases, the Police will routinely provide the 'S' (CHS)number, not the record itself. Staff should then obtain the record direct from the CHS.
>
> Source: Chapter 20: Criminal History Record: Police Officers. WWW.copfs.gov.uk/images/Documents/Prosecution_police

Esther looked forward to Christmas, especially this break. She was spending time with her 'princes.'. They did not have many presents, things were always hard after a court case, but they would eat well and be together.

Friday, Esther prepared their youngest son for his week with his father. He was sad, but she explained that this was just how it was, and once he got there, he would enjoy it. Off he went, Esther promising to see him in a weeks' time. She watched as he met his father, who was now pacing up and down the path, very preoccupied with His call. She thought 'He's calling the police again.' He would inform the court that their son had come down to Him late, 2 minutes past the time. They were none the wiser. There was nothing she could do, He gave information to the courts so that she could be viewed in the worse possible light. Their son had to walk down 4 flights of stairs 3 minutes pass contact time, 12 noon. Once their son got to Him, He spent time sitting in His car, writing up His notes, always at pick up and drop off times. Most Dads just wanted to get on with their contact times, to enjoy every minute He wrote notes for court, always looking for something to use as evidence.

Esther had vowed she would give Him no ammunition, so He never saw her at contact. However, when she appeared in court His outline to the court proceeding was unrecognisable. She was thankful her children were now older, and able to express a true account of contact.

'Out of the mouths of babes.'

A week without her baby was always hard, he was 9 years old now, but even after 5 years she had never gotten used to it, but it was fair that he spenl time with his father.

3 days later, Sunday, a text came though. *'Mum, there is someone at the front door.'* She was in church and quickly replied *'Don't answer the door.'* She was not expecting anyone, and her friends knew never to surprise her by visiting her unexpected. They knew she had to know who was coming to see her and when, so would call her beforehand. The frequent police visits unnerved her and the children, so any unexpected callers were greeted with Esther and the children looking at each and debating whether to answer it or not.

She couldn't cut her time in church, and it was her only way to relax, release and think about planning for the week. The praise and worship took her to another place altogether, away from her troubles, if only for an hour.

Esther returned home and hadn't yet taken off her shoes when the intercom buzzed. She answered it. She heard his sweet voice 'Mum, I'm home,' he was singing the words. She heart melted. She was so happy and let him in, unexpected but ever so welcome her 'baby' was home. She hugged him, trying to take in his usual smell.

> One child, we looked after became extremely upset when a teenager in the house used a particular aftershave because it reminded her …
>
> Source: The Girl who Just wanted to be loved Part 3 Google search 2020

He had sprayed him with His own aftershave, He did this, even though her son had asked Him not too. Esther couldn't understand why He kept doing this, especially as this could be problematic to their sons' asthma.

Her friend Euleen explained it 'He does it, so you smell Him.'

Esther was not upset or sick. She prepared the shower to remove the Aftershave in fear it would aggravate his eczema or asthma. She was numb to His games. Her only concern was managing her son's asthma. They had not attended A&E in 4 years.

He was hungry as usual. *'Dad told everyone you wanted me to come home.'*

Esther checked her emails, their only way of communicating for the past 5 years. He had emailed to say *'You should be here to meet _____ as you wanted all festivities re CE, CD, NYE, NYD.'* Sent from his iPhone. 00.20 pm.

She had not checked her emails that morning. She tried not to check as frequently when their son was at contact. It became a habit she had long stopped. She was not going to be controlled. Emergencies had occurred in the past, and He had taken their youngest son to A&E and given her very little information.

Esther had not sent Him an email since the 5th September 2019, 4 months previously. It was no point as He did exactly as He wanted, and she was now finding it impossible to communicate with Him.

2020 was coming, and she was definitely at her 'happy place' and made herself some promises she had to keep, one of them 'only necessary contact and hopefully in the very near future, no contact.' Her thoughts were interrupted.

'Mum, Dad called the police because you were not here to meet me.' Esther sighed. She called the police who confirmed that 2 CHS numbers were now against her.

Esther explained that on Friday, He arrived to collect their son, who needed time to walk down 2 flights of stairs and on Sunday, she was not aware He was returning their son home, as He was expected to have a week's contact time. The usual reply came.

'This is a civil matter that needed to be explained if this returned back to court.'

Esther now got it!!

The pattern had definitely changed, at any time they would return to court, and He raised the CHS number; the judge could access these details and see He had raised them against her! The goal posts had moved to allow any and all goals against her. She was in a goal with no way of defending it. The light bulb moment was so real. Her CAD numbers were just numbers on a page.

> The Professional Standards Directorate (PSD) is a small team of specialist investigators trained to deal with public complaint and misconduct matters. Staff are independent to the matters involving your complaint. The Directorate is an important part of the City of London Police.
>
> Source: Professional Standards Directorate – City of London Police

Esther wasn't accepting it this time and asked to make a complaint and was given a CAD number, and the matter was referred to the Duty Officer who called her back within 15 minutes. He took down the details and said her complaint would be passed onto the Department for Professional Standards. He assured her that her complaint would be investigated within 21 days. That was the end of December 2019: In June 2020, more than 6 months Esther had received no response to her complaint.

September 2020, no response to Esther's December 2019 complaint. This was exactly what Esther expected. No response.

'My Redeemer Lives' – Nicole Mullen powerful words, were what now allowed Esther time to reflect and cry in the stillness of the night. She had to let it out, and this was the only way she knew how. Esther felt defeated, going through this storm, she just couldn't see coming to an end.

> *"We May Encounter Many Defeats But We Must Not Be Defeated."*
>
> ~Maya Angelou

4th Campaign - **Legal**

Just Right Scotland
What Solicitors need to know about Domestic Abuse on May 14, 2018

Throughout the seminar, Helen highlighted that solicitors who work in this field have a duty to educate themselves on DA to ensure that they are best equipped to advise their clients. Helen acknowledged the increasing recognition of the scale and impact of DA in Scotland; however, more change is needed, and, in our legal system, change starts with solicitors.

Making Clients Safe

1. Listen carefully to clients, gathering both current and historical evidence of abuse (offering clients different methods to disclose information such as to write down what's happened or email it to then solicitor in order to reduce re-traumatisation)

2. Be knowledgeable about domestic abuse.

3. Take concerns of those affected seriously.

4. Listen to the client sympathetically and respond respectfully and sensitively

5. Remain mindful of the dangers that the victim has faced and may still face, assess the risk to a client -the most dangerous time for the client is often the point at which they leave; and

(To Be cont. . .)

> 6. Ensure that the culture of victim-blaming is challenged at the outset.
>
> Source: JustRight Scotland.org.UK
> Training for Solicitors, delivered by Helen Hughes

Esther was out of her depth; when the court summons arrived, she was not able to understand or even read them. She had prepared court documents for others but receiving her own court documents just sent her into a panic, and her emotions went into shutdown. She knew she had to go to court because He wanted to see the children, and He had alleged that she was stopping Him from seeing them. Esther knew this was untrue. His contacts totally suited His whimsical moods, agreeing to contact and Esther watching the children sitting and waiting only for Him not to show up. His visits were more reliable for their older son and his football activities.

> Your McKenzie friend is able to sit with you in court and offer advice and support as well as taking notes to help you. There are some things that a McKenzie friend cannot do on your behalf, such as conduct litigation, file court documents and statements etc.
>
> Source: mckenzie-friend.org.uk

Esther first attended court to seek legal representation. She was informed that she was not eligible to access a McKenzie friend, as this would be a conflict of interest. She had no idea what that meant. A conflict of whose interest? The person in the CAB (Citizens Advice Bureau) explained that the other party in the case had a McKenzie friend. Esther now understood.

> **Family need Fathers**
> **Aims and Objectives**
>
> Families Need Fathers is a registered UK charity which provides information and support to parents, including unmarried parents, of either sex. FNF is chiefly concerned with the problems of maintaining a child's relationship with both parents during and after family breakdown. Founded in 1974, FNF helps thousands of parents every year. The annual subscription cost less than a few minutes of a solicitor's time and gives access to a wide range of information and support that is beyond the scope of some lawyers.
>
> What we believe
>
> - Children have a right to a continuing loving relationship with both parents
> - Children need to be protected from the harm of losing contact with one parent
> - Both parents should be treated equally, and shared parenting should be encouraged
> - Each parent has a unique contribution to make to their children's development
> - The Family Courts should be backed by a nationally-funded mediation service
> - Litigation is not the preferred route for resolving post separation children's matters.
>
> Source: fnf.org.uk

Esther's first meeting with them, was at the top of Holborn Family court, in their contact suite. They introduced themselves as His McKenzie friend, they were thinking of the absolute best interest of the children's needs, and this was to have contact with two loving parents, Esther agreed. They informed her of their own personal background, Their son was denied contact with their children. The McKenzie Friend also worked for Families needed Fathers (FNF) Esther listened, making no comment, feeling a red flag raise within her.

They seemed friendly, in the beginning, listening to Esther's views and taking notes as they went on. She noticed that they would write her comments then draw a line and then write his own comments, the complete opposite of what she was saying, Esther, found this strange especially when she said He lived at his parents. The McKenzie wrote no and then wrote another area He lived. The McKenzie unconsciously was writing the truth down during their meeting. They continued to ask her questions and make notes. The meeting was going well until Esther mentioned that their oldest son did not want to spend time with his father. Their questions and their responses underwent a very different tone, and she felt more like she was being interrogated. *'Who is the parent here?' 'How old is he?' 'Can't you tell him what to do?', 'You are giving him too much choice and control?' 'He does not have a choice?*

With each question they threw at her, Esther protested. She could not make their son spend time with his father. Esther would explain the reason for their son's decision not to spend time, especially overnight, at his father's home. It was pointless. They were not listening. *'You won't win'* was their final verbal statement to Esther over the course of this and many more court dates.

Esther seized her opportunity; The McKenzie friend had left to talk to Him, and the Contact Supervisor of the suite entered the room to ask if she was ok. Esther asked if she could not talk to His McKenzie further? She advised Esther that the session could stop at any time. Esther did not wish to talk to them any further, and she asked the Contact Supervisor to tell them so. The Contact Supervisor did this straight away.

Esther wanted to cooperate, but their last comment had unnerved her. *'You won't win.'* Esther did not want to win. No one wins in a case involving children. Esther was never alone with His McKenzie, from their first meeting onwards.

Over the course of their numerous court dates, several other McKenzie friends supported Him in court, with one, in particular, being His main McKenzie representative. This McKenzie friend had a special need, and even though he was more than able to assist himself around the courtroom, He would hold their arm and guide the McKenzie into court. Esther found this laughable. He totally disregarded her own child who had special needs, she had seen His caring side, so this was a real facade to her.

Esther remembered the aims of FNF and His McKenzie worked for this organisation, and over the years would email His McKenzie to see if His disruption to contact could be avoided or if He could be reminded not to breach contact arrangements, to avoid the repeated court dates, further expenses and more importantly not to return the children to the court system. The responses she received made it clear His McKenzie was not willing to work for the good of the children.

> Parental Alienation is derived from parental alienation syndrome, a term introduced by Richard Gardner in 1985 to describe a suite of behaviour that he had observed consistently in children exposed to family separation or divorce whereby children rejected or showed unwarranted feelings towards one of their parents.
>
> Source: Parental alienation- Wikipedia

The reply Esther would receive was to remind her they were there to represent His needs only, nothing to do with the needs of children. Each of the emails she had sent were to inform them of the ongoing difficulties with contact with Him changing dates; not arriving on time; arriving on different dates; failing to return their son on time; not arriving at all; all issues that breach the court order. Esther would either be ignored, her emails referred to as 'tedious' or threatening to charge for their time: even when receiving an email saying He was watching them at the park, did not move them to help the children and her. Even more distressing was at each court date His McKenzie friend never mentioned His unreasonable behaviour or her continual emails to resolve each and every issue/incident. Their presentation always referred to Esther as breaching the order, and the statement of Parental Alienation was read out like a well-rehearsed line from an Agatha Christie play.

> 'They wouldn't tell a victim of burglary; Do you want us to do something about this? So why should that question be put to victims of domestic abuse? asks HMIC inspector.
>
> Police forces are allowing perpetrators of domestic violence to escape justice by ~"pushing responsibilities" for prosecutions on to victims, rather than building cases themselves, the police watchdog has warned.
>
> Officers need to "get on with their jobs" and track down evidence so they can pursue cases against offenders without relying on vulnerable victims to provide testimony, according to Zoe Billingham, who leads on domestic violence for Her Majesty's Inspectorate of Constabulary(HMIC).
>
> Source: Independent Article written by
Article Harriet Sunday
30 April 2017.

The police officer arrived to investigate damage to her car. She could not remember how many times her car had been damaged in some way or other – missing number plate, several punctured tyres, scratches down the side – Each reported but there was nothing anyone could do as there was no one to question. She saved each nail/screw taken from her car, an unusual amount, replacing a tyre every 3 months.

This was a police officer that treated Esther differently as he was taking down the report, unlike other officers that had attended her home. He watched her more intently when she answered. She thought he was trying to trip her up with his repetitive questioning. He finished, folded his notebook, thanked her for her time and left.

An hour later, Esther heard a knock on the door. She called out, *'Who is it?'* The intercom had not buzzed. It was the same police officer. She undid the door chain and opened the door. He stood there with a puzzled expression. Esther asked him quickly *'Was there a problem?'* He had just wanted to drop off a leaflet of where she might be able to get some help, The Refuge. She took the leaflet and looked at it. *'No, thank you'*, she said trying to hand it back to him. But he was walking away. *'Keep it. You may change your mind.'* She shut the door and placed the chain back onto the door. She had this feeling to check the officer had left the building and looked through the spyhole of her front door. The officer was standing at the top of the stairs, looking at her front door, with that same puzzled expression she had seen earlier.

Esther always locked the door, as it used to be each time they were at home, no matter what time of the day. Once inside the door chain was on. Now it could be anytime, once they were all at home. He had said He had posted all the keys back to her; she had never received them.

A Centre Run by the Refuge
How can the Centre help me?

- Talk to someone who understands what you are going through
- Receive support with contacting the police
- Move away from the area
- Access a refuge
- Stay at home, but want to find out how you can keep safe
- Receive support if you are considering going to court
- Access legal advice
- Manage your financial situation
- Find out about support networks in your community
- Get specialist support for your children

Source: Refuge.org.uk
0808 2000 247

She never really read through that leaflet until the court summons arrived. It was for The Refuge. There were offering legal advice for Domestic Violence victims. She was not sure how they could help her; she was only interested in getting help to keep her children. They could arrange free legal advice at their local centre.

Esther arrived at the centre; the Centre manager greeted her warmly, with a smile and an offer of a cup of tea. Esther refused; she needed to make this quick. She was only there just to get free legal advice, nothing else. The Centre manager understood, however, invited Esther to attend their weekly session, that had just started. Esther declined and repeated she was only there for the free legal advice. She had prepared previous court documents, but now it was getting serious. She wrongly assumed He just wanted access to the children. She had immediately agreed that He could have access to the children but had asked that He did not have access to her. This was ignored. She had to bring the children down to handover to Him. This was not enough. He now wanted the roles reversed - she was to see the children at weekends, and they now live with him. He had threatened her with this before saying He had someone in His family that could look after the children better than her. She needed help.

An appointment was booked for Esther to return the following week to see a solicitor; it was free for 30 minutes. Esther went home to prepare herself; she was awash with an enormous sense of relief; finally, she was not going to do this on her own. She needed to gather as much paperwork as possible.

A week later she attended the centre, long before the solicitor arrived. The solicitor was unable to attend. Esther could not contain her disappointment. The Centre Manager could see the panic and anxiety appear in her eyes. Esther, like her son, showed her emotions through her eyes. She reassured Esther that another appointment would be made as soon as possible. Esther was running out of time; the court case was looming nearer.

The Centre Manager suggested the solicitor's appointment could be brought sooner if Esther were prepared to attend the solicitor's office? Esther asked how much this would cost. The Centre Manager again reassured her it would remain the same, 30 minutes free legal consultation. Esther eagerly agreed and without hesitation.

Esther arrived at the solicitor's office, climbing the steep stairs. It was an old building, on the inside painted with cream walls, which very much needed a fresh lick of paint. Esther just prayed she could get some help for her children. The receptionist had her back positioned to Esther, as she entered the main door. Esther thought she recognised her, as she was speaking on the telephone when she turned around, Esther was correct. This was the most pleasant lady Esther had ever worked with, Ms J. She greeted Esther with a tight hug. She said she was not sure why Esther was here, but she hoped everything would be sorted out in her favour. Esther saw this as a positive sign of things to come.

The solicitor, a lady in her mid-thirties, dressed in a crisp black tailored suit, hair immaculately groomed with soft flowing black curls past her shoulders, had a cold and aloof manner, not turning in her chair. She had a stunning picture of, Esther assumed, her mother placed with pride on a shelf just above her desk. Esther stood awkwardly just inside her office door, not really wanting to enter, without being given permission to do so. She asked her to come in, and Esther again waited to be given permission to be seated. The solicitor beckoned Esther to sit down, with the flick of her hand, not looking up from her task. It was not really a greeting, just a motion of her hand, wavering towards the empty chair in front of her.

Esther perched on the soft upholstered seat. The solicitor asked how she could help her, her voice holding no emotions. There was no smile or warmth in her eyes, and the question delivered blunt and icy in tone and to the point. Esther began to explain her situation, marriage, separation, and the children court case at present.

A Very Civil Matter - Elaine Duffus

Please Don't Say! I sometimes don't know when He will stop

Don't say leave him?
Where would I go?
With my children, what do you know?
Who would put us up,
With no money guarantee
it will be a no show.
In the mess, I know but just listen to me
until I know how far can I go.

Why do you put up with it?
Tell me, the people that know, would you accept the consequences
– threats, terror, harassment, stalking or worse of all the thrashings
and beatings before I try to go.

Why don't you report him?
Will you be there when the authorities do nothing, and the beating
begins, or he takes away my children, with His lies and cabaret show?
Did not He deceive you and welcome you to His show.
The police will try to tell me they don't have enough evidence to
know,
So, to press this matter ahead, would be a waste of my toll.

Why don't you stop him seeing the children?
Tell me please when the children don't want to be missing their
father, oh no.
Stop asking me to get on with this person that plans, plots wanting
me to bend so low.

Instead, please help me to preserve within and my mind and my soul.

The children will rise and declare their own beautiful truth.

It's to break free of terror and be removed from His mould
At least you have a break from the children.
How is it a break when you fear when His patience is low
He's only taking them to increase His cash flow,

A break is more fulfilling with the knowledge that children are
treated with kindness, fondness and meaningful majestic love.

I never told you to leave him or judged you when you stayed, the days
He played away from home
I never said the words 'It should have been me',
' I would say do this or that.'

Believe it or not, Abuse isn't just physical; the psychological is harder
to shake from His invisible hold...

Please don't ask me these questions, I honestly don't know.

Instead, If you can't stop judging me, questioning me or listen to me
then please can you just leave me alone.

Elaine Duffus 8/11/16

The outburst that followed made Esther draw back. *'I can't understand why some of you women fall for these men and then end up giving them everything without the required plan or paperwork.'* Esther was unsure where or why She made this statement but sat in silence until She had finished Her rant. Esther needed help.

The solicitor then proceeded, now more calmly, *'Anyway I know of a solicitor who would be perfect for this case, but It will cost you, so let me locate her number.'* She turned and looked through her desk and gave Esther the details written on a post-it note, barely looking at her.

Esther rose quickly from the chair, thanking her before leaving the office. She walked straight down the stairs, past the receptionist area. She had promised to stop and say goodbye, but she just needed the fresh air of the busy high street.

Once outside, Esther looked at the piece of paper, folding it carefully. She placed it in her handbag. She became doubtful if she should call this number. What if she received the same negative reaction, she had just experienced? She walked home slowly, thinking. She had no choice; she was willing to accept anything to help her children. She never discussed with the support worker or the Centre manager at The Refuge, what just occurred.

> People will forget what you said …
>
> They will forget what you did, but people will never forget how you made them feel.
>
> Maya Angelou

Esther called the mobile number and spoke to the barrister that was going to change her and her children's life. As Esther spoke, the barrister listened, her response and advice was respectful, fair, honest and more importantly, genuine, advising Esther of the options available to the children and her. Esther was advised to cooperate with the whole process. He had a right to see the children. She was at all times to be reasonable. Esther gave extraordinarily little information of her own personal struggle with Him around contact, over the last few months and the last 4-year span of court dates. Esther felt it was not important or necessary to explain the dynamics of their relationship; the view was the needs of the children were paramount. Also, Esther did not want to bad-mouth Him, from her experience of Him and the courts, her opinion was worthless. Esther remained quiet.

Thousands of pounds later, the Child Arrangement Order was made with their oldest child not to have contact with his father and the youngest child to have contact, as arranged.

Esther was now heavy in debt, not paying her essential bills, and to be honest; she did not care. The fairness and respect with which this barrister treated her throughout the entire procedure wiped out the harshness of her experience with the first solicitor, and her skill in handling the various allegations was first class. Esther walked away financially broke but content that she had done the right thing.

> The world of Child Arrangement proceedings is uncomfortable, if not frightening and harmful, for survivors of domestic abuse. The adversarial nature of family court and the nature of domestic abuse means that survivors are almost certainly going to experience the following:
> Gaslighting
> Bureaucracy
> Lack of empathy from professionals
>
> Source: Full article available
> Domestic Abuse and the Family court 28th June 2019
> www.safelives.org.uk

He arrived at court with folders, pictures and witness statements to support His allegations that He had been abused, even being prepared to assert that the children had been abused in some way too; cuts and bruises that occurred at school, anything that He could add to His court statement to strengthen His case. Esther would be handed documents to read, when she arrived at court, after 10pm or early morning, giving her no time to prepare her response.

The court clerk informed her, she should have received them a couple of days before, but she learnt that many parents would deliberately give in their statements on the morning of the court hearing to leave the parent who needed to respond at a disadvantage. Esther never could get used to His allegations.

One of the many magistrates they sat before had asked them, *'Why don't you both just get on for the sake of the children.'* He automatically thought the magistrate was talking to Esther and looked at her nodding in agreement. Another of the 3 magistrates, noticing His gesture, leaned forward and addressed Esther, directly, *'You have done a wonderful job with both boys, especially your son entering in secondary school. Very well done, he has a place in this respected school.'*

He wasn't accepting or hearing the magistrate's positive statement to Esther. His email arrived, *'Did you hear what the judge said, it's not about you or me, it's about the children.'*

The contradictions, from the magistrates, on that day, confused and frustrated Esther. The differences of approach by the magistrates, even seated on the same court benches, produced different judgements and opinions. Some professional and some personal. Although they read the case files, they were missing the element of being present in the past court sessions. Esther felt this from the beginning at each new court date. Esther wished she had the consistency of the same magistrates as maybe, just maybe, the outcomes would have been different and possibly stopped Him for continuing these ongoing legal proceedings.

Esther reading through the documents at each court date over the months and years would go through a turbulent of emotions; sadness, shock, disgust, disbelief, helplessness, and finally shame.

She blinked at each court document, at His various requests in each court proceedings ranging from the boys attending the Parental Alienation Specialist Centre; to the children being placed into care, this would allow both of them to visit the children; James to live with Him to establish their relationship and their younger child remaining with the original contact arrangements, weekend, and holidays. With each and every document, she braced herself. His cruelness had no boundaries.

Esther prepared herself for the children to be taken from her because there was no way she would have them go into care. Esther would rather He had the boys', and she would not see them until they were older.

> **Children shouldn't have to sacrifice so that you can have the life you want. You make sacrifices so your children can have the life that they deserve.**

5th Campaign - **Football**

> Football United Against Domestic Violence is a campaign by Women's aid, working with national footballing bodies, sports media, football clubs, the police, players, and fans to send a clear message that domestic violence is always unacceptable. Together we aim to call out sexist behaviour.
>
> Source: Women's aid.org.uk

Esther's mother had decided she could not take her grandson 'mashing up her place.' Esther was told to find him a football club. Esther laughed and explained she couldn't afford it. She had left Him, and money was non-existent, for extra social activities for their son. Her mother ordered her to find a club, and she would pay whatever it costs, and anyway *'My boys going to be a footballer man.'*

Esther didn't know where to start. She Googled everything, so that is where she started. She discovered there was a football training club locally that she could take him to. She called them and found there was space to start that coming summer holidays. She arrived at football summer camp, and James was over the moon, his dream to play football were about to begin.

Esther registered him, and the coach asked whether he was any good. Esther replied and said she didn't know, explaining he also played Saturday football and they did not think her son was good enough to be picked for their team, which had disappointed him. James lived and breathed football. She would hide the football, and he would play with a rolled-up sock or anything else he could find to kick and something else that could be used as a goal post. He would get upset when his favourite team lost, or players transferred. His life was football and all it entailed, plus it was high time for both her and her mum to have a break from items getting broken.

Esther hugged him and checked what time she needed to collect him. She stood watching him for a short time and once she was sure he was fine, walked away. As she looked back, she saw that he hadn't even noticed she had gone. Esther returned at 4 pm. The coach asked if she would stay behind, and automatically, she wondered what he had broken. She gave him the side eye. He was just smiling, ecstatically happy, with a week of football, from morning to afternoon. Everyone had now left, and the coach pulled up two chairs for them to talk.

'He's good.' He confirmed and asking her son's age. He was visibly surprised. Esther was used to this reaction; he was tall for his age; hence no one believed the age he was. The coach would like to give their son extra training sessions to develop him further then move him to trial at the local academy club. Now Esther was surprised, 'move to an academy', what did that mean? She would Google it. Esther did not want to ask in case the coach thought she was stupid.

He had told her for years *'You don't know anything about football.'* His words rang in her mind.

Esther explained again, her son attended a Saturday club, and he had never been picked for matches as they said he wasn't good enough yet. The coach laughed and totally disagreed.

He wanted to meet her son on Sundays so that he could be trained at another boy's home. Esther wasn't sure, and she would need to think about it; she knew immediately her son would not be attending without a parent. Esther could not take any chances of him coming to any harm.

The coach, seemingly reading her mind, reassured her it was safe and asked her to think it over during the summer camp sessions and they could discuss this further. He then asked, as if to check, if her son was coming to the camp over the summer? Esther said she would try for him to attend as much as possible, explaining her mum was paying for the sessions. The coach agreed this was a good solution to give him further training while Esther made up her mind. She still was unsure about her son going to a stranger's home, someone had to go with him, and she saw no way she could do this with her other commitments.

She told her mum, who was excited, *'I told you my grandson going to be a footballer man.'* Esther was not sure; this was a lot to add to her already heavy workload. Her son saw this an opportunity to ask his grandmother for new boots; without hesitation, his grandmother gave him the money.

Esther was trying not to exclude Him from their son's activities, so told Him of the coach's proposal and the new training. He agreed to attend one of his sessions, promptly reminding her, He knew more about football, and she did not. Esther knew it would come; her lack of knowledge was used as a sharpe knife to nudge her back into her place.

> ### "I am depressed."
>
> Rafael Nadal. Nadal wrote in 'Rafa: My story' that his parents' split was devastating. "They were the mainstay of my life, and that pillar had crumbled. I was depressed; I lacked enthusiasm. I had lost all love for life,".
>
> Source: essentiallysport.com
> Rafal Nadal's Parents' Divorce – Did it Affect Rafa Performance.
> By Varun Khanna December 26, 2016

He arrived and walked past her and stood on the other side of the field. Esther stood there, astonished by His action. She could not recall any disputes or disagreements. He publicly showing her His ice-cold face and behind a closed door, trying to have them reconciled; when this failed then Esther was shown another side, far worse, Hate and Dismissal.

The coach noticed this and after the session commented *'Players do better when their parents get on even if they are apart. They do even better if they are together'*. Their son was unhappy and embarrassed that his parents lived apart, referring to this several time over the summer camp period. Esther recanted her decision. She felt they should give it a couple of months of being amicable to each other to start. Everyone was happy but her, she ignored all and any of the negative comments He made, *'I knew you would need me for this,'* '*You don't know anything about football.'*

To the outside world, He was the attentive husband and father showing care and interest in their sons' talent. He returned from His first meeting with the coach, to take their son to the Sunday training sessions, complaining He lacked finance to do this, the child maintenance should cover this. Esther gave James his 'snacks monies'. At the end of summer camp, the coach said their son was ready to be sent over on trial to the local academy.

Esther thought it was just for a few training sessions a week. She was wrong – 2 sessions a week, training with the other team and matches. No, she was not prepared and could not do this on her own. He reminded that this was their son's future and if he did not attend, this would be her fault. She was obliged to do what she could, but it was hard and a struggle to fulfil this commitment.

After a few sessions, a coach from a local grassroots club approached Esther to ask if their son could join their team. The fees were not affordable, but again her mother helped to pay. He was unable to pay as He *'did not live with them'* and had to cover His living costs.

Their son needed 'game time', and Esther did not have a clue what that meant, but He was happy to tell her in detail. He made her feel her lack of football knowledge would hold their son back, and she needed Him to be there; however the clause was that she had to fund it and to attend when He was working, this was not negotiable. Esther did not want to commit to this activity, her foremost priority was caring for her Mum and then the children's needs, her own personal needs did not even come into the picture at this point.

Their son was ecstatic that he was being taken to football; it was everything he had dreamed of.

His constant reminders that He was unable to financially contribute to this additional activity as He *'did not live with them'*, reinforced the guilt He wanted her to feel; He reminded Esther that if she did not do this, *'She was holding back their son's future.'* Esther was struggling to pay for everything, and He refused to buy his football boots, cover petrol costs, buy extra snacks, anything to do with the additional expense, everything had to be paid out of Child Maintenance, that was what it was there for, the children needs. He expected Esther to learn to make the money last for the month and cover everything. He would then turn up at all the games playing the proud father, shaking everyone's hand and standing on the side-lines inspecting their son's performance. His grandiose sense of importance was a sight to behold.

Esther did not want to do it; she was just too tired. The times she could not take their son to training would result in an onslaught of abuse. She was *'Lazy'*, *'Not committed'*, *'She was holding their son back.'* Esther forced herself to do all what she could and with her mother's help and encouragement.

Esther had a true love for football, and although she did not know every rule, more importantly, she loved that this was the one thing that their son loved too. She watched him on the pitch, and he would look her way, and she knew he was happy even if it was only for the 30 – 40 minutes on the pitch.

> The former Leicester and England player Legend Gary Lineker has condemned pushy parents in an outspoken article.
>
> The former Foxes striker and father of four described the behaviour of competitive mothers and fathers as utterly depressing and warned it is hindering their children's competitive development as players. . . . . . .
>
> He admitted he had felt compelled to speak to fathers on the touchline at matches to try to get them to calm down. In the past, he has spoken of witnessing parents swearing at referees and shouting at their own children during games.
>
> Source: Foxes Talk. Gary Lineker tells pushy parents to shut up. By DavieG 24 October 2013 in General Football and Sport

The competitiveness from particular parents was fierce, and the thing that bothered Esther was the cruelty of some of the parents, snide comments at the side-lines were unbelievable, and with not a care for the mental harm they could cause a young athlete. Esther could not understand, these boys were as young as 7/8, but you would think they were fully paid Premiership football players.

Esther knew this added pressure on her son, and after being told their separation should not be open knowledge amongst the other parents, and the academy was not in their sons' best interest, she felt embroiled in an impossible situation. Esther watched her son on the pitch, totally focused and nothing or no one mattered.

Esther was under pressure to sign the contract for their talented son, aged 8. The Academy Coach had put on an impressive PowerPoint presentation outlining their son's potential, which took place in the actual premiership stadium, which they both attended, the facade had to be maintained.

He was overwhelmed and had no hesitation in signing the contract.

Esther could see no way to make this work. He began the name-calling as soon as they left the meeting, *'lazy'* being His main insult to throw at her. He was working, and she was not, so as far as He was concerned, she had no excuse to not do everything for their son's future. When she attempted to protest that she had other children, He was quick to remind her that her first child was not His concern and their young son could be left with her mother, regardless of the fact that she was aged 87 and not well. Esther didn't respond; it was pointless when His mind was set. Their son was on his way to a promising career and no one, especially her, was going to stand in His way, it was His son's future. Esther saw an 8-year-old having fun, and He saw the next Thierry Henry fully dressed in the Arsenal kit.

Esther decided not to mention this to her mother; she had to think about this, her mother would say do it, even if she was left alone, and this was not always possible. Esther was not sure how this was going to be managed. Their youngest was under 2 years old with ongoing medical issues that meant he might need to go to the hospital, if not managed properly; her mother was not well, and her older son had additional needs.

Esther's mother carried on regardless, but she could see her mother was hiding how unwell she really was. With everything together, this was just not manageable. He wouldn't hear of it, and He was fuming as He spat out the words *'This is not about you or me'*.

He was bringing their son home from one of the many evenings training sessions, arriving with their son carrying a brown parcel, beautifully secured with string. Their son ran in, shouting as he headed straight to his bedroom, *'I have a surprise for you, Mummy.'* James returned to the lounge, dressed in the full academy kit.

Esther protested they hadn't signed the contract. He was not happy; she had spoilt their son's moment and ignored her. Their son was beaming; this was his dream. They both looked at her. She went to her desk and signed the contract. She told Him He would need to look at changing His shift. She couldn't do it. He agreed, waving his hand, to dismiss her. He would go into work and have all His shifts changed. This never happened.

If Esther ever said she was unable to take their son training, or to a match, the verbal assault was severe.

Esther was not sure about other cultures, but what she had observed in her own with some friends and family, especially the older generation, if you did not work, in some way, then you were *'lazy'* and leaving it all on *'their poor husbands.'* There was no considering what that mother did during the day or who she was looking after. The wife had to work, hitting the workplace even after the birth of a child. The husband could be fine with his wife being at home, but the extended family, especially in-laws, would ask the question. *'when are you going back to work,'* even before the baby was born.

Esther would be subjected to abuse by text, *'lazy'*, *'bad mum'*, He would also include His discussion with His family and what they thought of Her. *'They all think you are a lazy mum.'* She attended out of guilt each time; she looked at their son in his kit, which he wore with pride, she knew she had to work out a plan to take him, on her own, but not just now.

> For some families being under one roof does not work. The stress of long hours, commitments and strains can impact on their family life and no matter how hard the parents work at trying to keep the family unit together they can't. Separation happens, and whenever it does, it can be a good thing for an unhappy family who knows being apart is the best thing for their children. It can also bring relief to their children.
>
> Source: divorce.wikivorce.com written by Naomi Richards

No one was supposed to know they were separated; she did not think it was any of their business.

Esther had an older son before her marriage, and with his father, they attended all events, both social and educational together. On one occasion, she had mentioned to the teacher that they were not together and on leaving the meeting, her ex-partner gently reminded her that this was none of their business, and she was duly corrected.

Esther had finally made it clear she did not think they should be together, and He saw this as His sign to make it public, walking pass her at every opportunity, training or matches, making a point to kiss all the mothers and shaking the hands of all the fathers, but openly ignoring her. At first, they looked at her puzzled and shocked. Esther informed them they were no longer together. Their initial reaction was to encourage them to get back together; they had never fathomed; they were not together from the beginning of their son's football journey. Once their 'business was out', Esther found there were more parents that were separated than she had realised, and some who wished they were separated, especially the woman paying the bulk of the expenses in their homes. They stayed together for the sake of their children; it was easier. The difference with them is that they kept their private lives just that, private.

Their situation embarrassed their son, who was now not wanting his father to attend, walking a different route to get to her to avoid meeting his father. Now Esther was being blamed for that. When His father began to attend with His family members, who had never attended before and their relationship with Esther was non-existent, this escalated their son to further not wanting his father to attend. The extended family attempting to give their son instructions from the side-lines, also saw their son reluctant to attend matches.

Esther felt uncomfortable, but this was His son also, and there was truly little she could do. When He and His entourage arrived, she would retreat to her car until the match finished. Esther and their son planned before the game, that if He and his family members arrived,

Esther would move away. Their older son would know where she was parked and would come to her.

> Being made to feel worthless. There are lots of signs that point to an abusive relationship. The one we want to talk about here is not visible but probably the most indicative. It's being made to feel worthless. Consciously or unconsciously, that sense of worthlessness is what abusers are always trying to instil in their victims. We say consciously……
>
> Source: Abuser Try To Shift The 'Victims'
> By Michael Schreiner June 20, 2017

Esther was now completing the majority of training and matches with James, and He would now at the very last-minute send a text to say he was stuck at work and she would have to do the football activity. Esther was in exactly the impossible position she wanted to avoid. Esther informed the academy she could not do it anymore. He was furious, informing her they had signed a contract and she had to do it. Esther refused; this was not her only commitment. He had renamed her '*Lazy*' whenever she refused.

> Gaslighting is a form of psychological manipulation in which a person or group covertly sows seeds of doubt in targeted individual, making them questions their own memory, perception, or judgement, often evoking in them cognitive dissonance and other changes such as low self-esteem.
>
> Source: Wikipedia.org
>
> **Where did the term 'gaslighting' come from?**
>
> The term "gaslighting" comes from a 1938 stage play called Gaslight, in which a husband attempts to drive his wife crazy by dimming the lights in their home{which were powered by gas), then denied that the lights change when the wife asks him about them.
>
> Source: Gaslight 1938 British Stage Play.

His constant reminders that Esther was holding back their son by not attending to all his activities due to her 'laziness.' Further confirming His family held this opinion of her also. Esther wasn't working and the car He had given her as a 'birthday gift' (that she paid for monthly) was to be solely used to take their son to football. He had now asked for the car to be repossessed, by the finance company, informing her it was her fault. Esther was still expected to find a way to do this and every other activity with their son, even getting on the bus. Esther tried to do everything she could to get her son to the academy, at all costs. She felt a great sense of failing her son whenever she was unable to do this and started to take on what He said that she was, *'lazy'*; after all, she was not working.

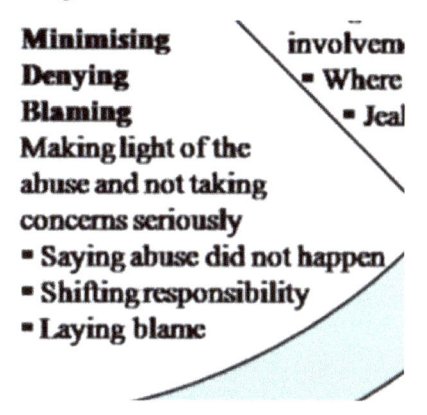

Minimising
Denying
Blaming
Making light of the
abuse and not taking
concerns seriously
▪ Saying abuse did not happen
▪ Shifting responsibility
▪ Laying blame

involvem
▪ Where
▪ Jeal

The local Academy's Coach did not want their son to leave and arranged a meeting to see them both to discuss how they could help. Esther and the head coach sat in the café, awaiting His arrival. The Head coach received a text. He was not attending the meeting. The Head coach looked embarrassed and apologised for Him not attending the meeting, to discuss their son staying at the academy. There was nothing more to say. Esther informed the Head Coach of her position - she was now not able to continue both football and private education, financially. She was doing this on her own. His financial contribution was just that; it did not cover the added expense of football costs. Esther's priority was her son's education. The Head academy coach suggested they could move her son to a good state school they were affiliated with. The Head academy coach felt that it would be good for her son and he would be able to continue with the football. Esther refused, in her mind, thought what a blasted cheek – football over education! Esther later researched the school mentioned, and she found it was of a poor Ofsted rating.

His abuse and accusations by text continued, and Esther was left to either take their son or have a very distressed child. She sat their son down and explained that she would not be able to take him to all the training and matches, as she had to look after his Nan. Their son was understanding but visibly upset.

He never changed his shifts to accommodate the hectic football schedule and if He did arrive at training and matches and their son was not present, Esther would most definitely receive the texts telling her exactly what kind of mother He thought she was.

Esther had arranged with the academy to do as much as she could until the winter break; then she would use this time to think. Esther also decided to have their son take time off from his local team to recharge from the hectic last 4 months. They all needed the rest during the Christmas period. Her mother was now very unwell, and she needed to spend more time with her. The texts of accusations came consistently; *'You are ruining my son's future, 'just because you didn't make it, you don't want my son to make it.'* Esther couldn't budge, even if she wanted to, everyone needed some rest, and she had to think about how this was going to be managed in the future.

He had contacted mediation, Esther welcomed this as a sign some arrangements of contact could be established. It was agreed that He would undertake the football activities. He attended for the first week's training sessions and then called their son's school informing them He would not be picking their son up, as He had important work training to attend for the next 6 weeks. He never mentioned this at any of the mediation sessions whilst making all the contact agreement, even agreeing He would be able to speak to His manager so these necessary arrangements could be put into place. Esther could not leave her mum for lengthy periods, so she asked for a local team coach to pick up their son and take him to training; she had to look after her mum. Frankly, she would not leave her mum.

The following week He agreed to pick up their son if Esther did the drop-off. Esther saw this would work if He did some of the routines; Relieved, she dropped off their son and returned to her mum. It was later than usual for their son to return home. He was not answering His phone. Esther was getting worried. She heard a knock and went to answer it. Their son had been returned by another parent. He had called the other parent to say He was stuck at work and could they take their son home? Esther thanked the parent.

He sent a text much later to apologise. Their son had been scared, not seeing his dad; he had panicked and become upset. Esther just hugged him; this was not the first time he had left their son at a football event.

The Football Association Recommended Guidelines

Statement of intent
We are committed to providing a caring, friendly, safe environment for all of our members so they can participate in football in a relaxed and secure atmosphere. If bullying does occur, all club members or parents should be able to tell and know that incidents will be dealt with promptly and effectively. We are a Telling club. This means that anyone who knows that bullying is happening is expected to tell the Club Welfare Officer or any committee member. This club is committed to playing its part to teach players to treat each other with respect.

Source: Anti-Bullying Policy for Football Clubs. Respect. TheFA.com/Football safe

The bullying of their son by a few boys in the locker room was increasing. The teasing and taunting was seen as 'Boys being boys.' Esther complained frequently to the academy. Their son was now unhappy to attend with his father. He could not understand why his father was hugging, greeting, and kissing the parents of the same boys that was bullying him in the locker room. Each time Esther asked about the bullying, He denied it and put it down to her 'babying' their son, and this was 'Football'. Esther disagreed.

Their son returned from the pitch visibly upset. Esther knew just by looking at him something had happened. He sat in the car. *'Mum, he called me the 'B' word, in training".* Esther asked her son to explain what had happened. Her son explained no one wanted to pass the ball to him, and when he had the ball and did not pass it to a particular boy, the boy called him the 'B' word. Esther jumped out of her car and went directly to the lead coach of that age group to complain. His excuse was automatically to defend their favourite player, *'He travelled far to attend their academy, he was tired; however, they would talk to him,'.* What followed was to make Esther very much aware that this matter was not going to be taken with any seriousness. The lead coach continued, *'Maybe your separation is causing your son to be sensitive to comments.'* Esther explained that her son was not used to being sworn at by his own teammates and no, this was not due to the marital separation, the separation had taken place before he arrived at the academy, so he was now very much used to their situation. Esther was not tolerating their excuses.

The lead coach said he understood, as He had recently separated from His wife and child. He was paying maintenance, and she didn't need it as she (his wife) earned more than Him. Esther listened in amazement, hearing the bitterness in His voice. The lead coach was telling her His problems. Esther was now thinking He most definitely was unsympathetic to her situation.

From that day, onwards Esther always placed all her concerns and any incidents, in writing to the academy, she had to keep an ongoing log as the situation was deteriorating. They preferred not to put anything in writing, asking Esther instead to attend meetings to discuss concerns. Esther had previously attended a lot of meetings where there was no follow up actions to any of her concerns about her son being bullied. The situation was worsening, the boys concerned realising there was no consequences increased bullying her son. Their parents became involved by sending Esther to 'Coventry' – deliberately ostracising her; not talking to her, avoiding her and acting as if she did not exist.

He saw nothing wrong, *'It's all part of football'* was His statement, especially enjoying that the parents did not speak to her, and when He did attend, would make a point to walk past her and stand with these parents.

Esther could see her son becoming more withdrawn from the sport he had once loved and was now making excuses not to attend. Before her son would try to attend every training or match, ignoring any sickness symptoms, now he would remain in bed quickly giving in to the 'stomach or headache'.

> ### WhYD7 are these YD7 and YD10 forms?
>
> If a young person leaves an Academy, he and his parents will be given one of these forms to sign, and the termination will be recorded forever and a day on either YD7 release or a YD10 release. The former is better known as a release 'without compensation', whereas the latter is a release 'with compensation'.
>
> So where are the problems?
>
> I have come across the following scenarios:
>
> Club A allegedly told the player and his parents that they would not be extending his registration verbally, but in a letter made an offer to extend which the parents alleged they never received. The player/parents reacted to verbal rejection and were asked to sign a 'release' form. They were given and signed a form YD10 and sometime later discovered the relevance of this when after

> a successful trial Club B wished to register the player. Club A sought compensation and relied upon their letter and YD10 form.
>
> The parents were adamant that their son had been told he was being released verbally and that they signed the 'release' form put in front of them on face value.
>
> Source: Fullcontactlaw.co.uk By Dan Chapman

Esther waited in line to speak with the lead coach, after a match. Before she could say anything, He demanded she take her son out the academy. She asked the lead coach to confirm this in writing. He ignored her, and she watched as He walked onto the pitch and bought her son over to her telling her *'He can leave now.'* Esther asked him, *'Are you releasing him.'* He said 'Yes.' The coach for her son's age group stepped in and disagreed. Her son was now embarrassed; Esther was disappointed. All of this was taking place in full view of other parents of the academy and visiting academy parents and families. This was the same coach who had complained of His wife demanding child maintenance. Her son was not released from that academy. The lead coach made a point of barely talking to her son, and when Esther did attend activities, He would make a point of walking pass Esther and her son and shake hands with his father's hand, at every opportunity.

Years later Esther was sent a WhatsApp message about the lead coach, who had made her son and her life at the academy, so difficult; He had resigned from the academy amid allegations of him making a racial slur, to a member of the public.

> **Dealing with Bullying on Youth Sport Teams**
>
> When you sign your kids up for sports, you expect them to have fun, get some exercise and learn some new skills. But nothing is more heartbreaking than discovering that your child sports activities are being overshadowed by bullying. Whether it is the coach bullying your child or one of his teammates, the experience can be devastating.
>
> Source: Very Well, family by Sherry Gordon updated on April 11, 2020.

Esther's mother had died, and nothing was getting easier. Esther really did not want to be around anyone much less parents, and their unkindness, at football activities.

His inconsistency was letting their son down with His no-show at training and matches and the subsequent Child Arrangement Order, now allowing their son not to attend contact, saw Esther doing all training/matches. He continually reminded her that she would never be able to do it all, especially driving on the motorway to matches. He reminded her of her weakness.

> Emotional, Verbal or Psychological Abuse: name calling, put-downs, humiliations, jealousy, mind games, making the victim feel crazy, making the victim feel bad about her/himself, making the victim feel as though they are to blame, and comments such as 'No one will ever love you as much as I do," "No one will ever believe you," "and "You're so stupid, fat 'etc.
>
> Source:New-hope.org

Esther needed help and asked her nephew, to do the driving – long distance or locally – to matches. Esther was now able to ask anything of him, and his knowledge of football saw her now learning the art of football; getting her head around the offside rule was a huge step forward. Esther attended as much as she could, but she just didn't want to do this alone anymore.

> It's not the lie that bothers me it's the fact that you knew it was a lie and you kept your silence.
>
> Elaine Duffus

Esther noticed the 'look and nod' she received from certain parents when she arrived with her nephew but thought nothing of this, at first. A mother who knew her well pulled her aside to ask, 'Who's that?' beaming. Esther called her nephew over and introduced him. The parent looked uneasy and a little disappointed. She explained that there was a rumour that Esther's nephew was, in fact, her new partner, but she wouldn't say who had started that rumour. The saddest part was that there was another parent who knew Esther and her nephew and yet never corrected the 'rumour' stating it was not his business, and he did not want to be involved.

> If your partner is cheating, they may display some of the classic signs, such as hiding their phone, staying out later than usual, or making drastic changes to their appearance. But once you get suspicious, they may add another layer on top of it all, by attempting to manipulate you into believing they're not cheating.
> To do so, they may gaslight you, blame you for the problems in your relationship or make you out be the cheater –
>
> Source: 11 Signs Your Partner Is Manipulating You Into Believing They're Not Cheating/ By Carolyn Steber Oct. 11, 2018

Esther dreaded attending court, as at each appearance His court statement would be filled with accusations, and this time was no exception. She was being accused of attending their son's events with her 'boyfriend.' She denied it, and the judge settled the matter firmly looking at Him. *'Whether she has a partner or not is totally irrelevant to this case and quite frankly is no one's business.'*

He would subsequently accuse her of being intimately involved with various males Esther had contact with especially young football coaches, that trained their son. Each time this occurred in court, Esther would have feelings of shame, humiliation and sadness. She never remembered the judge's statement *'It was irrelevant to the case,'* just the thought it was mentioned embarrassed her.

Match day arrived, and her son woke up and got himself ready, he was noticeably quiet, making an excuse he was not hungry, he skipped breakfast. Esther knew this was unusual. They began to walk down the stairs. Her son stopped, *'I'm not going back.'* Esther didn't question this; she was surprised her son had lasted this long. The bullying was fierce with specific boys making cruel comments about him not having the latest name branded boots; she couldn't afford them. The continual court appearances meant that she was unable to afford to buy her son new boots every season; her mum, was no longer around to help. They laughed at her son, making him feel he was not good enough. When specific boys teased him, the others would laugh. Her son's love of football held him at this academy, but after the passing of his Nan, Esther had seen a noticeable change.

He blamed her for messing up their son's chances. Esther hadn't noticed that their son didn't smile or laugh. He wasn't allowed to go to the park, like other little boys, and play on the climbing frame. He would say, *'He could get hurt'*. He wasn't allowed to ride a bike, even though he had 2 bikes nor even learn to swim.

> What I had perhaps not envisaged at the time was quite how many parents of young players – through no fault of their own – found themselves in dispute. Worse still, how their parents (and also clubs seeking to register young players) found nowhere to turn, nowhere to seek advice or remedy and often left no choice but to resort to drastic measures to salvage their young son's chance of a football career.
>
> Source: The Curious YD forms? By Dan Chapman
> www.fullcontactlaw.co.uk

Esther signed the YD10, for her son to be released from the local academy. She was not to know that years later the devastating effect her signing this form would have on her son, she should have sort further legal advice.

Esther noticed over the months how relaxed her son had become, uncurling his toes, not biting his nails and knuckles. His whole aura became easy-going and happy. Her son smiled, and she could hear him laugh often, she couldn't remember the last time he had laughed. His character as the joker of the house was coming to light.

Her son always blamed himself for being too eager to play for an academy, but Esther always reassures him it was her responsibility to be stronger and not sign the forms, he was too young and should have been allowed just to enjoy playing football.

> *"Success is no accident. It is hard work, perseverance, learning, studying, sacrifice and most of all, love of what you are doing or learning to do"*
>
> ~Pele

6th Campaign - **The Church**

> Abusers work hard to isolate those they're abusing by threatening, discrediting, or shaming them into thinking nobody will believe them.
>
> Source: The Gospel coalition.
> How to combat Domestic Violence in the Church
> Written by Mark Spaniel January 5, 2106

Esther was attending an event she was particularly looking forward to, she had not put on a dress for the longest time and glamming up was something she rarely did; the boys were already in their traditional Tuxedo and were equally excited. The night was going well; it was a truly spectacular evening and beautifully organised.

As the event drew to it's close, a young lady appeared, with a guest book, for people to sign and write their thanks and best wishes to the Hostess for the evening. The young woman arrived at Esther's table and deliberately walked pass her to approach another guest, at the same table to sign the guest book. The other guests observed but made no comment. Typical, Esther thought, no one says a thing about rudeness, especially at a church event. *'Everyone see and blind'*, was the saying that sprang to Esther's mind. She smiled, maybe years ago it would have hurt, but now she was in a different place and considering her life, she was nonchalant to the opinion of others or how they saw her. Her son watched and sent her a questioning look. Esther shook her head to indicate not to worry. He had seen the disrespect and wondered why it had happened. He watched her wherever she went and was ready to come to her defence if need be.

> 'One child may be acutely aware of the abuse and may take on the role of family protector. Their siblings may refuse to acknowledge it at all.'
> Source: Children and family: How can you share parenting with an abusive parent? The Guardian Jess Hill
> Sat 14th Mar 2020

In the past, their older son had done just that, trying to shield her. Esther shook her head again, this time more firmly, to reassure her son, she was fine. She watched him settle back against his seat, but he was still observing, in case anything occurred.

Esther initially did not remember that something had happened years previously, with this young lady. At home, James asked her why that lady had been so rude. Still, Esther could not recall. This often happened, when an event was not important to Esther, she would block it out.

The next morning, she rose early to pray and then she remembered.

An inappropriate relationship could have been formed. Esther saw the passing of a telephone number, on a slip of paper, as it sailed across her path and landed onto the older man's lap. He scooped it up quickly but not quick enough. Esther informed the leadership. The man was much older than the woman, both of course strongly denied this had occurred. They were believed, and Esther was not believed. Both parties were wounded that they could be accused of such a thing and anything Esther said after this was questionable. Esther remained at her church for several years later.

He decided He would join Esther at her church and from the very first visit was welcomed with open arms, His sense of humour, charm and always being willing to help make Him a hit with all who met Him. He was given a senior position, and Esther was seen to support His role. He reminded her of this constantly, pointing out her length of time in church and how He had arrived and was immediately given a promotion. He was 'Blessed and Highly favoured', and He would say this and leave it hanging in the air.

> 'A woman I'll call 'Marlene' went to her pastor for help. 'My husband is abusing me,' she told him. 'Last week, he knocked me down and kicked me. He broke one of my ribs.
>
> 'Marlene's pastor was sympathetic. He prayed with 'Marlene' and then sent her home. 'Try to more submissive.'
>
> Two weeks later, 'Marlene' was dead – killed by her abusive husband. Her church could not believe it. 'Marlene's husband was a Sunday school teacher and deacon. How could he do such a thing?
>
> Source: Domestic violence within the Church: The Ugly Truth church

Esther attended every reconciliation meeting and agreed to anything and everything. She wanted her marriage to work. He reminded her that *'She had never really loved Him'*, *'You are making the father of your children homeless'*, *'No one would believe you'*. Esther was spoken to by senior leaders to try to make it work, as all marriages go through 'a bad patch.' He was holding His own court, with a Pastor who supported a men's only ministries.

> Thousands of parents falsely claim domestic abuse in order to access legal aid and stop estranged partners from seeing their children, a shared parenting charity claim
>
> Source: BBC News by Hannah Richardson, BBC News education and social affairs reporter 3rd July 2018

Esther was constantly being reminded she was in the wrong, 'You are the black cloud in this marriage'. She shouldn't have put her hand on Him. He made no mention that He and His family members were threatening or verbally abusive to her. She knew her mistake, she should have called the police before going inside.

There are 3 sides to every story – His side, Esther's side and The Truth. His side was believed, especially due to His position.

Esther accepted her punishment, she was wrong, and for her punishment, she was to stay with Him. She had fought back, and that was wrong and gave Him ammunition, a golden ticket to tell everyone the problem lay with her. Esther never realised that this was the green light for Him to do or say absolutely anything.

> There are special guidelines on marriage in the church if you are divorced. There may well be a way forward, but you will need to talk to your Vicar about your situation to explore the possibilities for you.
>
> Documents you'll need
> if you are divorced, you will need to bring your decree absolute for the vicar to see.
>
> Source: Legal requirements. www.yourchurchwedding.org

Court documents arrived, Esther immediately noticed the inaccuracy. She knew Him well enough to realise He was going to jump on this serious error. She was correct, and His accusations began within days. Esther contacted her solicitor to ask that the court documents be amended, but it was too late they had already been sent out. Esther asked her to amend them regardless. The solicitor agreed to send an amended document. Esther was untroubled by what He thought of her, what concerned her was that it was totally untrue.

> 'A reputation once broken may possibly be repaired, but the world will always keep their eyes on the spot, where the crack was'.
>
> Joseph Hall

She was ready for the accusations if they were to come into court. His next move was totally unexpected, and it came to wound her character and reputation.

The telephone call came from One of the Leaders. Esther had a great deal of respect for this leader as he was like a father-figure to her, always kind and giving her the utmost respect, even when he corrected her. She always left their conversation feeling valued and appreciated. He began to inquire how the children were and then how she was doing, the conversation was strained, and as she replied, she never anticipated the real motive for the call. They had never had a strained conversation, and this felt laboured. He coughed, Esther waited, it was coming.

'Were you married before?' Esther composed herself, thinking back to errors in the court documents and His accusations of her lying about her past.

As Esther had anticipated, He had immediately picked up on the error, and the accusations began. She had informed Him that her solicitor had made the error in the court documentation. He wouldn't hear of it, of course, Esther had lied to the church that she and her previous partner had not been married. Esther reassured Him that if that were the case, she would have had to produce a Decree Absolute. He insisted she was lying, and if this was the case, their marriage was not legal. Esther knew this was untrue and told Him so, and she felt she had to insist on this point to one of her Leaders from church, she had never been married before.

Esther felt an overwhelming sense of betrayal and a huge sense of shame.

She knew she would not have hidden that even if she had been married to her ex-partner. There were together for over 10 years since Esther was 19 and their relationship was nothing like this, they had just grown apart and moved on in their respective lives. Their co-parenting of their son had worked for 12 years.

Esther confirmed she was not married and explained the solicitor's assumption and error. They ended the telephone conversation with the usual pleasantries, but Esther knew instinctively things had changed, and for a strange reason, she felt she was not believed.

> The one who throws the stone forgets, the one who is hit remembers forever.
>
> African Proverb

As the court date approached, to decide a marriage separation, He approached her. His persuasion was smooth. *'I want us to try again, and I forgive you.' 'We are so good together.' 'I'm your husband, and always will be.' 'I was angry because I thought you didn't love me anymore.'* He hugged her, and she felt safe. First, The Hook, and everything He had put her through in their first round of court dates, was forgiven but the hurt remained.

How to Have a Trial Separation In the Same House

Can you be separated and live in the same house? Seems an impossible task unless you know how to go about it. Trial separations happen in marriages, and contrary to popular belief, they don't always spell the end of a relationship.

So, exactly what is a trial separation?

A trial separation means that two parties have decided to take a break in their relationship and to use their time apart to decide whether they want to continue working at the relationship.

Source: Marriage.com by Sylvia Smith, Expert Blogger
Approved by Angela Welch, LMFT
Updated: 28 Apr 2020

The courts agreed with their decision; they were separated; however, they would live under the same roof. Esther knew this was not what she wanted, but their oldest son wanted this father. She was uneasy. His statements in His court documents were cruel and untrue. She couldn't forget, as they replayed in her mind, but she was taught to forgive. He saw her uncertainty and attempted to dispel her doubts, *'I didn't mean it'*. Esther's solicitor wanted to know for sure that Esther had made the right decision, asking several times, if Esther was sure she wanted to live with Him, she expressed her personal opinion of not trusting Him. His accusations and allegations disturbed her; saying these things against His own wife made her wonder what else He could do. Esther talked herself into believing that everything would be fine, but she had this uncomfortable feeling deep down; dismissing it, she persuaded herself she had to try, the children were happy, and everyone at church was joyful, they were working at their marriage. No one was any the wiser of the previous bitter court details or their now living arrangements. But Esther knew as each day went by, she became more and more regretful and despondent with the situation. He began with making her breakfast in bed, looking after the kids with no problems. They attended church, and everything looked as it had before. The perfectly turned out family.

A couple of weeks had passed, and He stopped attending church with Esther and the children, making excuses, and preferring to remain at home. Esther was relieved, as this was her time to reflect and think, knowing she was coming to the end of her marriage but was just unsure how to end it. Esther had experienced wanting to leave Him and seen the lengths He would go to not only destroy her mentally and financially, but spiritually, and what she saw was frightening.

On her return from church, He would begin the same questions / accusations, *'Did anyone ask for me?' 'It's your church anyway they don't miss me'*, *'Did you send another one of your letters?'* Esther was truthful, He was always asked for, and this seemed to add to His importance.

Pausing to think, *'Sending a letter, what letter?'* she asked. He laughed *'Don't go on like you don't know.'* Esther did not have a clue what He was referring to. He exaggerated His laughter by throwing His head back, '*The letters you sent to my family*'. Esther looked puzzled. He walked away, shaking His head. '*Shameful.*'

Esther was left baffled with this statement.

Esther never realised that His ongoing non-attendance at church helped to forge the stories He was painting of the 'abused husband' unable to leave the house, not wanting to show His 'afflictions.' As the weeks passed Esther began to notice that certain people were avoiding her. She mentioned it to Him, and He told her she was 'paranoid.'

At home He wouldn't eat anything she cooked, distancing Himself, only talking in brief words or sentences, sending messages through their son or ignoring her completely.

Esther's answer came when she went to greet the Pastor who had His own Men's Ministry, and He walked straight pass her and the children, His wife, made a hasty cover-up, by greeting Esther with a warm embrace. Esther knew now for sure that He had said something. Esther called the Pastor's home and spoke to His wife, asking for a direct meeting. She agreed to '*come back to her with an answer.*' They never returned Esther's call. Esther asked Him to arrange a meeting for them both, to sit with them and receive counselling. He laughed saying '*He won't meet with you.*' It was confirmed.

Esther was silent. Where was she to go for help now? This was the church she had attended for over 10 years, and if one of the leaders did not believe her, then maybe the others did not either?

> 'There ain't a man in the world cares about a woman's past until he's thinking of her in his future.'
> Dru Pagliassotti

Esther attendance to church was becoming more difficult, with the feeling of her past 'alleged' marriage, used with anything else He could say she had done, topped off with His barrage of insults and abuse each time she returned home.

One day a visiting preacher gave the word(message) that if a wife hit her husband, she was wrong. Esther stopped attending church completely. She was ashamed, and He had won. She was no longer a Christian. She had heard the message and told Him. He gloated *'I told you God don't sleep and will never listen to you.'* He quoted His favourite scriptures, *'No weapon formed against me shall ever prosper,' 'I am the head and not the tail.'* And His all-time preferred scripture was printed on a t-shirt, *'I am blessed"*, worn to be her reminder.

Esther ventured out only to attend to necessary appointments and to speak only to who she had to. If anyone from church called she would answer but give an excuse – she was feeling unwell, the children weren't well, she didn't have money to drive all that way, and her go-to excuse, she had to look after her mum. This went on for months, then a Pastor that Esther was close to was having no more excuses, asking her directly, why she was not coming to church? Esther was silent. She reminded her that whatever she had done, she should just go to God about it. Esther made no reply; she just listened. The pastor talked and talked and talked. Esther listened and then cried. The pastor again asked, *'What's the matter?'*

> ### "Reactive Abuse"
>
> They call you abusive for reacting to their abuse.
>
> Aspect of psychological abuse and manipulation is for the abuser to claim that the victim is being abusive towards them. I've written about the abuser's "victim complex", and "gaslighting."
>
> A good way to recognise a victim who had reacted to abuse, and a psychologically abusive person creating a smear campaign, is their attitude towards their actions.
>
> Victims will almost always be able to admit their fault. They will know they reacted badly and did wrong. This quality is actually what the abuser usually holds against them in the first place to make them believe they are the ones in the wrong.
>
> Abusers will almost never admit they have done anything wrong. Their victims will be blamed for everything.
>
> Source: The Minds Journal May 2, 2017.

'I hit him.' Esther whispered it. *'I was wrong.'*

'Why?'

Esther explained He said she was wrong, and she had to be punished for what she did. How could she go to church after what she had done?

The pastor asked again, *'Tell me what happened? and why? I know you love him. Why?'*

Esther was silent; there was no excuse. He had explained *'If she loved Him then she was simply wrong'*. She agreed.

The Pastor asked again. *'Why did you hit Him?'*

Esther whispered, *'I tried to get Him out, but He won't leave.'* Esther cried.

The pastor attempted to continue the conversation, but Esther made the excuse that one of the children needed her attention. The pastor said she would call back. Esther avoided her calls.

Esther had accepted this was how her marriage was going to be. She would be reminded whenever she said no. He would remind her that she owed Him. If He arrived with £100 trainers, she had no right to say anything; after all, He was justified in making Himself happy. It was His money to do with as He pleased. The children's needs were not His problem; nappies, baby milk, food for the children, household bills. As far has He saw it, Esther had mistreated Him, and His 'people' believed He was entitled to compensation, especially as He now had other things to pay, that was more important.

Esther avoided talking to her closest friends and family; they would know something was wrong if she contacted them. She had no idea He was calling and visiting as many friends and family, even her own friends and family, to vilify her. His contact with His family which He had limited previously was now more frequent, visits almost every day. This Esther welcomed, as their home felt at peace without Him. Esther hoped that He would decide not to return.

In the darkness of night, she heard His key turn in the lock, He had returned making as much noise as possible, wanting to make His presence felt, with little regard for the sleeping children. Esther did not care; she would sleep when He was at work in the day.

> ### 6 Signs He's Playing The Victim To Destroy You
>
> Victim playing is a kind of emotional manipulation men use to keep you around, to break you or simply because they truly believe that they are victims.
>
> It's the kind of manipulation we quite often brush off because they really have convincing stories, and how could a victim be a manipulator? But its manipulation, after all, so watch out for these signs and excuses that he might be using on you.
>
> !. Every ex He had was a @***@
> 2. You are always attacking Him
> 3. He dumps all of His problems on you
> 4. He turns tiny incidents into arguments
> 5. He doesn't seem to understand
> 6. He Never feels the need to apologise.
>
> Source: Further reading on this article herway.net
> Tatiana Belikov 2 years ago

He arrived from work in an unusually quiet mood. He usually found a fault to argue about as He entered. Nothing she did was right, and He was continuing not to eat with the family. Esther noticed He was in the same clothing for the last 4 days. He had access to everything, food and a shower, but He refused to use either.

He began the conversation casually, *'Who have you been talking to, today?'* She found this strange. He had not spoken to her for days, No Hello or goodbye and still used their son to pass messages to her. Esther avoided being in the room with Him and retreated to the bedroom. She was okay there.

'No one.' She answered, unsure where this was going.

He laughed *'Well, I know who your friends are.'* Esther went to leave the room as He said this. He followed her. She had not noticed that their older son had already left the room. As she reached outside her bedroom, their son called her, *'Mum'*. She headed straight into his bedroom.

He had turned and was headed away from her, mumbling to Himself. Their son was protecting her; he had seen what was about to happen and headed out of the room. Esther had not even noticed he had left the lounge, calling her into his room to protect her.

Esther was tired, finding it hard to sleep when He was at home, and when she did fall asleep, any movement or sound awakened her. She had catnaps, and when He was at work would catch a couple of hours when the baby had his nap.

The arrangements were that she would have the bedroom and He would sleep in the lounge. However, His clothing was in the bedroom, and He would find any excuse to enter the bedroom, using the time to ignite an argument or accuse her of something. He waited for the children to fall asleep and entered the bedroom.

'You moved my stuff', throwing His bag onto the side of the bed, just missing the baby who was also sleeping next to her. She thought having the baby lying next to her would deter Him from doing anything. Esther jumped up to defend. He held up his chin, *'Go on, I know you want to.'*

Everything immediately became clear, He wanted her to react again. He was goading her; she lay back down, drawing the baby closer to her chest. This was too easy.

> **Women three times more likely to be arrested for domestic violence**
>
> While the vast majority of perpetrators of domestic violence are men, women are arrested in three of every 10 incidents and men in only one of 10, a study says.
>
> Men are responsible for most cases of domestic violence, but women are three times more likely to be arrested for incidents of abuse, research reveals today
>
> Source: TheGuardian.com written Staff and agencies
> Fri 28 Aug 2009 11.10 BST

He leaned over her. *'You can't help yourself. Smashing my stuff and telling everyone I'm bad. But no one believes you. Your friends and family know what you're like; you can't control your temper. That's why your ex chose someone better and younger than you.'*

Esther watched Him and remained silent. He moved closer and again, sticking out His chin. She knew she would lose the most precious things to her, her children. He was not worth it

He turned and immediately rang His Mum. *'She hit me'*, looking straight at her.

Esther looked at Him, amazed and shouted so She could hear her, *'No, I didn't.'* She knew it was pointless. He replied *'Told you she's always shouting at me in here and now she's going to wake the kids .'* Esther remained silent; this was exactly what He wanted.

Esther lay still as He walked away, His plan was not working as he hoped, she was thinking - Why had His mother not asked Him to come home? Then she remembered the wedding day, His Father asking back for their house key and another instruction, *'If anything goes wrong do not come back.'*

> Abusers use everyone and everything around them in a manipulative way, including their children as tools of abuse.
>
> Source: healthy place.com by Sam Vaknin

Esther knew she could not bear much more of this. He was doing exactly as He pleased, and their oldest son was allowed to do anything – playing football in the lounge, staying up late, feeding their youngest son anything He ate, regardless of his allergies. Esther endured anything, as she knew she could not rise to His bait. Her love for her older son from a previous relationship was indescribable, and He knew this. He changed His tactics to ramp up the pressure on her.

He would become annoyed if her son moved His keys, asking her, *'Why is he touching my things?'* Esther would not reply and just put back the items her son had moved. He was aware that her son had additional needs and liked everything in its correct place. His habit in the past had been to return from work and place his keys on the bookcase shelf, now He would throw His keys on the dining table; her son would move them to the place He had kept them for the last 7 years, the bookshelf. Esther knew it was an excuse to create an argument and would retreat to her room and whenever possible, leave her older son at his father's home.

> **Sleep Deprivation Used as Abuse Tactic**
> Domestic Violence survivors often find they have trouble sleeping. Being abused and controlled by one's partner hardly equates to a restful night's sleep.
>
> Source: Domesticshelter.org written by Amanda Kippert Oct 10, 2018.

Esther had to spend time with her mum, this was the only time she felt at peace, and she could in no way allow her mum to know how bad things really were, the sheer worry would not help with her illness. The only time Esther could just relax and more importantly, sleep, was laying on her mum's bed. She was finding it hard to sleep when He was around as she was unsure when He would wake her, accusing her of anything and everything. If the slightest thing was moved, He saw it as her trying to cause trouble with Him.

It was time to go back, and she sighed, she went to the car and tried to start it, no petrol. In over 15 years of being a driver, Esther had never run out of petrol, but her finances were low. She did not want to ask her mum; she would then know things were not as they seemed. Esther would have to call Him to collect them. This she was not looking forward to.

He sounded polite on the phone and agreed to collect the children and her. She hurried to get the children ready before He arrived. He hated to wait downstairs and saw anything she asked Him to do as an inconvenience. She knew the polite tone on the phone was not what she would receive when He arrived. Esther knew He was in the company of others when He spoke to her this way.

He arrived. *'Why didn't you ask your mum for money?'* Esther didn't reply. She placed the children in His car and told him she would get the bus and meet them at home. She knew, by the way, He laughed He was going to say something to goad her. *'Bus? If you get the bus, I will take my children to my mum's.'* He had set the bait. He knew Esther would get into the car. It was late, and the boys needed to go to bed.

> One in 4 women live in destructive relationships, and many of these women sit in church. Every day, next to the abuser, the father of their children.
> Source: Fact sand trends.net
> written by Aaron Earls – October 25, 2018

The drive home was agonizing, He played gospel music and would sing how blessed He was. Esther sensed there was trouble, He was very happy. She asked Him to go to His parents for the evening as she didn't want to argue. He laughed, like always. They arrived home, she ran out of the car, grabbing the 2 children and quickly shut the front door, their oldest son instinctively moving as quickly, if not faster than her. He ran to the door, and she shouted for Him to go to His parents. He was silent. Esther looked out the lounge window to see Him walk to the driver side of His car.

Their older son looked at her, looking like he was going to cry. She knew something was wrong.

'Mum, I forgot my school bag.' Esther's heart sank. She called out to Him to drop the school bag at the door. He told her to come and get it. She asked him again to drop the bag at the door. He stood outside His driver's side. Esther thought she would have enough time; He was at the driver's side of the car, she could quickly run out and grab the school bag from the front seat.

> Between 3 and 10 million children (depending upon the study will witness domestic violence in this country this year. The majority of children who live in homes where there is domestic violence have observed the violence at least once (75 -87%, depending on the study).
>
> Source: Facts & Myths – Child Witness to Violence Project

She would have to take that chance, she ran. He arrived at the passenger side exactly when she did. The door came against her with such a force. Esther mustered all her strength, to push the car door and Him away. The pain she felt was excruciating; her right upper arm felt numb from the impact of the car door against her. He saw that other people were walking towards them and began to hold his head, staggering back, shouting out with pain, 'She hit me.' He sat on a wall with His hands-on His head. Esther didn't care what He was saying, the fear outweighed the pain she was feeling, and she ran as fast as she could inside, holding the school bag.

James was standing at the front door; She was not sure for how long, he helped her inside. She locked the door. He was not coming back in here, she had decided, she just couldn't take anymore.

'Mum, what's that?'

'What, baby?'

James picked up her phone and directing Esther to stand up, asking his mum to hold her right arm up. Click. He handed her phone back to her. Esther had found her decisive factor; she would never be with Him again.

She gazed into James' eyes that day, He was worried and scared, and she knew then that was the end of her marriage.

The phone calls came from leaders of the church – to arrange meetings with them both, to think of the children, to reconsider the finances – stop CMS, He had nowhere to go, it's His family, etc. The pastor pleaded with her to tell the leaders what was happening. Esther remained silent.

> It's almost auto-signature for churches today: "All Are Welcome!" And the impulse is a good one. For centuries, the church has been exclusive rather than inclusive, despite Jesus' desire to the contrary. We have excluded women, African Americans, immigrants, gays and lesbians, people with special needs, senior citizens, singles, 20-somethings – at times; the church has been downright discriminatory.
>
> Source: Sojo.net
> Written by Angela Denker Nov 11, 2014.

He had now been away from them a while, and she felt it was time to return back to church. Her pastor would always give her encouraging words which helped, always ending with *'Do the right thing'* or such kind and gentle words as *'You haven't done anything so bad that God will not love and forgive you'*, this helped Esther to go back to her first love – God.

> Abusers tend to act secretly. They will not abuse the next-door neighbour openly or be offensive and abusive to their boss. They will put on a pleasant manner when meeting with people they want to impress- people they do not want to have find them out. The two-faced nature of abusers, in itself, makes it harder for their victims to speak out.
>
> Source: Psychologytoday.com Darlene Lancer June 06, 2017.

Esther was so swept up in the Praise and Worship music, her favourite part of the service; she could feel the essence of every single note the musicians were playing, just for an hour, she could forget everything.

He had arrived and was making His way towards them, James began to cry, alerting Esther. He was embracing everyone as He approached them. She stiffened and felt sick. Their youngest son jumped out of her arms and ran to Him. He called James to come to Him, but he was frozen to his chair and leaned closer to her. He threw up His arms in a 'whatever' attitude and walked with the only child that wanted to be with Him. James looked petrified. They knew when He 'flicked' His hand this could be the ramification of something unpleasant and embarrassing – verbal or emotional repercussions. Esther looked at her son, the dark circles around his eyes were prominent, his skin looked pale and patchy, the corners of his mouth drooped. She looked in his eyes and saw fear. Esther remembered this is how the children looked when they were first taken into care and removed from their parents. She wanted to scream 'how had she not seen this before?'

Two elders of the church gently took James, who had begun to cry openly, using another door, so he would not have to walk past his father. He sat at the back, helping the sound technician, rocking their youngest son. Esther knew she had to leave, but He had the 'baby.' An elder returned asking what she wanted to do?

'What about the baby?' they reassured her both boys were now together in a room at the back of the church. They held her hand, leading her

out of the middle door. He noticed she was leaving and rose to leave out of the back door of the church hall. She ran pass Him to the room the children were in. An elder stopped her. *'You can't leave like this.'*

Esther was frantic and thought, *'Why can't they just let us leave?'* He had now taken out His phone and was filming her, trying to leave and being held by one of the elders. Esther calmed immediately. She knew this would not look good at court, all evidence that could be used against her, seeming erratic and having someone in church holding her. Esther moved out of His view and into the room the children were.

> You may meet families at church, or the park and they appear to be 'the perfect family.' Abused wives, their controlling husbands and children are beautiful, well kept, dressed nicely, hair perfect, always smiling, always saying the right things, but behind the four walls of their home, their life is completely different.
>
> Source: The Abusive Marriage Stories of 3 Abused Wives and their Controlling Husbands. WWW.domestic-volence-help.org

The two elders looked at her, then one spoke. *'The boys have told us.'* Esther looked quickly at both boys. She in no way wanted anyone to know what was going on

The pastor spoke *'I knew before the boys told me. Esther, it's time to talk to the leadership.'*

Esther was now beyond caring; she just needed to leave and get to her mum's, her safe place, She won't be believed, anyhow they all liked Him and what He had told them would be deemed as the true version.

Esther asked them to allow her 15 minutes; then if He wanted to leave, she had a head start. She felt like a hunted animal. They went to leave, and He was standing outside the door waiting. They walked past Him. He leaned towards James to hug him, James stiffened and did not hug Him back, leaving his arms limp at his side. James' eyes sent her messages if he was hungry, sad, frightened, then his eyes told her everything. They rushed to the upstairs car park and drove away.

> Abusers use everyone and everything around them in a manipulative way, including using their children as tools of abuse.
> The abuser often recruits his children to do his bidding. He uses them to tempt, convince, communicate, threaten, and otherwise manipulate his target, ...
>
> Source:Healthyplace.com

Once they had driven for a while, James spoke. *'Dad said to make sure your mum doesn't scratch my car.'* No one had heard Him say this even though there were Elders less than a foot away from Him. Esther decided she had to move to another church, Her faith was not something she could give up, but she couldn't continue there.

That evening one of the Elders called to see how her and the boys were. Esther was fine. The Elder then explained that she had given Him a lift back to South London. He had not driven, His car was playing up, but He just felt the need to attend church. Esther was stunned. He had purposely attended church because they were attending. She couldn't understand why He, the alleged victim, would want to be present at any event she was present at. He had always reminded her it was her church, as she was a member years before He joined. But what worried her more was how He knew the children and her, were at church that day? He attended with no car, taking train and several buses.

She remembered previously the technician had tried to talk to her at her car to let Him see the children, explaining His own situation with His children and the breakup of His marriage. Esther had cut Him short by moving away. He had not approached her again and if possible, avoided her.

> An abused wife is slowly being beaten down so low that they live in total fear of their husbands. Abusive men isolate their wives and make them put on a cheery exterior when they are out in public, but behind the four walls of their home, violence and cruelty is happening.
>
> Source: www.domestic-violence-help.org

Years earlier, Esther, another member of the church and the technician's wife were in discussion, when the technician arrived and became involved in the conversation. It became awkward, as it was just mums having a chat. But what made this conversation more uneasy was in mid-sentence He leaned back to talk to Esther - She was totally unaware of what He was going to say - *'Can you give my wife some advice on how to do her hair? Your hair always looks nice.'* He was referring to His own wife, who was standing right there with them. He didn't whisper it or even try to hide what He was saying. It was plain for those in the group to hear, making His wife uncomfortable. He said it as simple as though he would ask for a coffee, without a thought or care as to how His wife would feel. Esther leaned forward making no reply, unsure whether to defend His wife or ignore His question altogether. Looking at His wife, she chose to ignore it.

Esther was so troubled by how this man treated His wife and expressed her concerns to her friend Lorna. Due to His position in the church, Esther did not wish to offend this family, and it was possible maybe she herself was wrong and had misread the situation. It appeared to Esther that He would seem to blame His wife if the children were not prepared adequately for church, while He arrived looking sleek and perfectly groomed. His wife and the children would arrive a little flustered and dishevelled. Esther had noted when picking up their baby that his Babygro was too small, and his toes were constricted. They decided to be practical as there was no proof of anything untoward and the only visible sign was the children's lack in practical areas. They both would contribute to a basket of items for the children – clothes, nappies, etc. It was decided that Lorna would drop off their gift, as she lived nearest. The gift was delivered, and although the concerns remained, between them, there was little more, they could do, other than, if possible, bless the children with gifts. The matter was not discussed after that day.

Sunday arrived, and both Esther and Lorna was separately spoken to regarding their 'gift'. The technician had brought this matter to the attention of leadership, and He felt they were implying He was unable to provide for His family and it was felt that in future any 'gifts' should go through the church. Esther and Lorna were extremely upset but more annoyed, this was in no way intended to offend His ability to provide for His family. Esther really could not understand why He was so offended with them giving gifts to their children. She was puzzled. However, He had succeeded, they made no more contact with His wife, even in the church, she would make every effort to avoid Esther and Lorna. He had planted the seed that they were questioning how He provided for His family, and they were interfering in His role of head of His house. Lorna was reassuring, *'We know our intentions were for good not bad. We must stand in our own truth.'*

At the time, Esther was just upset for being seen as interfering, even gossiping, about His role, as head of His home. Esther had always been known as the person that gave gifts; she just loved to give.

On reflection, Esther now she knew His intentions and His tactics was to isolate His wife.

> Emotional Abuse: Identifying Spiritual Abusiveness in Marriage
>
> ### What is the connection between emotional abuse and spiritual abuse?
>
> A subtle form (or not a subtle depending on how you look at it) of emotional abuse sometimes experienced within marriage is spiritual abusiveness. The idea of spiritual abuse is a foreign concept to many people. So, what is it, and how does it become emotional abuse?
>
> When it comes to abuse, remember, all abuse (including emotional abuse), is based on power and control as opposed to love and respect.
>
> So, spiritual abuse occurs when a leader, or in the case of marriage when a spouse attempts to control, manipulate, or dominate another person, this is emotional abuse. It is often lurking under the guise of someone who is "being religious."
>
> Additionally, guilt and shame are effective weapons for the abusive party in controlling the victim.
> Obviously, this is emotional abuse too.
>
> Source: Emotional Abuse: Identifying Spiritual Abusiveness in Marriage
> www.madaboutmarriage.com
> Posted by Mike Tucker November 9, 2011.

She had made her decision, regrettably returning was not an option, and He was aware of her routine on Sundays if she were to continue. He decided it was her church so He would leave, but she knew He wouldn't stick to this, turning up when He felt the need to 'see the children'. There was a possibility He might arrive at any time, and Esther could not take the chance for the children and her to experience His presence again.

Esther wrote her letter of resignation to the Leadership, her sense of loss and grief was profound, as this was the church, she had attended the best part of 17+ years. The very place her faith and self-esteem grew. She was given responsibilities and loved to work within the International, Women's and Children's Ministry projects. He was given a title, and this was always a reminder of how highly the Leadership thought of Him, and that Esther's attendance all those years was meaningless.

The pastor continued to call Esther regularly to pray and check that she and the boys were doing okay. She would before the end of each telephone conversation, ask how Esther's finances were. Esther would say they were fine, but the pastor would automatically remind her that she wanted to make sure her *'godson needed for nothing,'* and they always end with praying. A deposit was made into her account that evening.

Months past, the pastor approached the subject, as Esther was not coming back to church, then she needed to fellowship somewhere else. Esther agreed and began attending the local church. She was familiar with them as her mother had attended for over 20 years; they knew nothing of her past and, more importantly, He did not know what church she attended. The boys complained they missed 'their church' – the songs, Sunday school, their Godmothers, everything. Esther agreed and promised to find another church, but for now, she just had to attend a church. She was not going to let Him win using the argument that God did not forgive or love her. The guilt would rise up at the most unexpected times, but she continued to attend a church.

He sent His reminders via His WhatsApp profile, and when the courts were shown His profile posts it was granted all correspondences should be emails only, He was unable to send His concealed messages via His WhatsApp profile. His main quote being, *'No weapon formed against me shall prosper'.*

> ## Trying to Communicate with An Abuser
>
> "It's like he can't hear me."
> "He makes me feel like I'm crazy."
> "When I try to talk to him, he treats me like I'm his enemy."
> These are some of the things abuse victims might say when they share with me how they try to communicate with their abuser.
> I want those of you who can empathize with those sentiments to understand that there is no real misunderstanding. The man hears you, he wants you to feel crazy, and it's not surprising that he is treating you like you are his enemy, because that's pretty much the way he sees you.
>
> Source: Trying to communicate with an abuser.
By Cindy Burrell,
March 20, 2019.

A year had passed, a couple of days after New Year's day, she received His email.

'Told you I would always be welcomed.'

Esther did not understand and frankly cared very little for His random statements. She tried to begin this New Year, trying to not engage with the constant negative correspondences, she'd had enough of communicating with Him. Her hoping He would just stop was a pointless expectation.

It was now approaching a year her mother had passed, and it wasn't getting any easier losing her. January was a difficult month.

A friend telephoned her and began by apologizing, Esther was confused. He had arrived doing His usual meet and greet, at church. He was welcomed back with great applause from Headship, pleased to see Him, as when someone was welcomed if they were visiting or had been absent for a long time. After the service, He walked around embracing all He could. He surprised her friend with a hug. She was sorry but more annoyed with herself as He had caught her off guard. Esther reassured her not to worry, He had notified her He had attended and of His great welcome. Her friend was surprised and corrected His version of that day. He was greeted, and people were pleased to see Him however there was by no means great applause from everyone, and He had walked around trying to find people to talk to Him at length and then eventually left. Esther felt uncomfortable. She in no way wanted anyone to not talk to Him. Their friend explained how weird it was after nearly a year He just arrived at church. Esther told her about His email, where He said everyone hugged Him. The friend again corrected His version. No, everyone had not embraced Him, and in fact, He had embraced some that did not wish to be embraced.

> If I could describe the impact and aftermath of emotional abuse in one word, it would be 'invisible'. Emotional abuse may leave no physical marks, but the depth of the scars and the weight of the pain creates a burden that people can't see - or don't want to.
>
> Source: Returning Yourself After an Emotionally Abusive Relationship by Sophia Stephens on Tuesday, November 27th, 2018.

Her brother rang. He was a year older than her and very quietly spoken. Esther admired her brother as nothing phased him. He was exactly as you saw him, gentle and kind. He had been a born-again Christian since the age of 19. Regardless of what life had thrown him, he accepted and changed it to a positive, and he was a man of his word, always optimistic, ready to give a positive word of encouragement to everyone, even the people that were unkind to him. He was 'a man after God's own heart.' He trusted God's process and the plan was unshakable in all situations.

He was her rock, especially when their mother had passed away. Esther had completed lost control, crying all the time, just not functioning, he kept her loved and grounded. To others, he seemed aloof, but someone had to be in control to organise everything, and he was. Esther always felt immediately calm in his presence, either by his WhatsApp messages to her, telephone conversation or when he visited. They didn't see or speak as often, but their closeness was unmistakable, she knew he was always at the end of the telephone to discuss anything. The distance made no difference; she always felt loved and respected by her brother.

The conversation began with general questions, and then he asked, *'Why have you not gone back to church?'* They had danced around this subject for nearly a year now. Esther had made sure not to give her brother her reasons. She respected her brother and did not want him to know what she had done. She told him and waited, his answer bought her the instant relief she needed.

'I love you sis, but more importantly, God loves you. You need to be in fellowship. Don't listen to anyone that tells you that you cannot be forgiven. You really need to find a church that feeds your spirit.' Her brother wouldn't say a bad word against anyone. Esther knew but more importantly felt he was right; she had felt this for months, she now needed to move to a church that suited the style of worship she had experienced and enjoyed for the last 17 years. She agreed with him and would remain where she was for now but look at visiting other churches in the meantime.

> "Out of all the things that you deserve, self-forgiveness is towards the top of the list."
>
> Sophia Stephens

Esther received many invitations over the years to visit church events, even from her old church, but she had this feeling of not feeling worthy to attend. Her decision to attend this church just felt right. On arrival, this church was different, the feeling of peace and calm was immediately felt, she had never anticipated that this would be her spiritual home, but the boys and her were settled.

His emails never stopped coming reminding her of her mistakes, attempting to make her feel guilty, but she took her brother's main advice, which was simply, *'Don't reply. You are feeding Him. Men do not like it when you don't reply to them.'* Esther had heard this so many times, but the explanation coming from a man, it just clicked for her.

The children were all asleep, and Esther had to think. She had never imagined leaving her old church, and she just sat still listening to Marvin Sapp, *'Never would have made it without You'*. Esther knew without her faith; she couldn't do it now or in the future.

> "In the end, we will remember not the words of our enemies, but the silence of our friends."
>
> Martin Luther Jr

7th Campaign - **Refuge Centre**

Refuge - The Gaia Centre

> The pioneering Gaia Centre, funded by the London Borough of Lambeth, was the first of its kind in the UK to offer a 'single point of access for women, girls and men experiencing violence and abuse.
>
> Source: Refuge.org.uk

Esther had initially only attended because the police officer had said they gave free legal advice. His past threats to permanently take the children away, report her to social services accusing her of not caring for her older son together with the ongoing court appearances had drawn her to attend the centre. Her grandniece had expressed her concerns, *'I'm worried about Aunty E.'* gave the much-needed wake-up call to seek help.

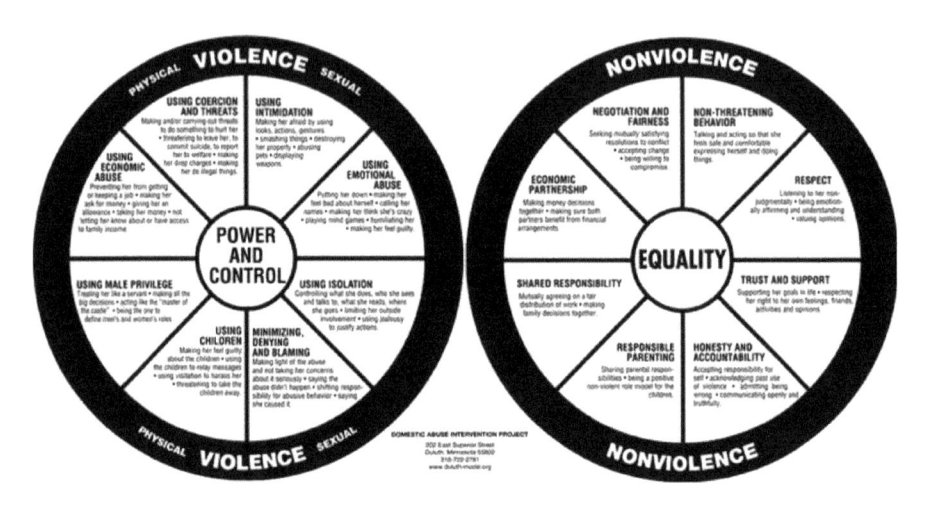

For the first couple of meetings, Esther felt out of place, making no eye contact and not speaking with anyone. This situation she was in was real, and she was not in it alone. The Power and Control Wheel shocked her into a position of raw truth. Her present situation was covered in every section of the power and control wheel, and her previous relationship covering the opposite, the equality wheel. She had left Him, but it made no difference, the situation was just as fresh and painfully raw as if she had stayed with Him, waiting for the next mortal combat to begin. She was in a 'war', a victim of unforeseen circumstances, the helplessness overwhelmed her.

It was now months on, and she rushed to attend the session. She had another purpose for leaving her home and attending the sessions, other than the children's needs. The sessions she attended were conducted by different organisations that encouraged abused women to build on their self-esteem, wellbeing and gain new skills or rediscover existing skills. Who would have thought she could write? His words rang in her ears – *lazy, dumb, stupid* – she had to remind herself who she was before she met Him – smart, intelligent, kind, generous, and each session validated this. She was stronger when her mother was here, but now, she was different and attending this session allowed her to recall her gift, a love of reading and writing, other than court documents.

Esther walked with purpose to this particular session, taking the straight walk down Coldhabour Lane, preferring to walk instead of taking the 2 buses. This gave her permission to think and take notice of the area she lived in for over 40 years of her life. It was absolutely beautiful; the smells and vibrancy of Brixton filled her with energy. She had a couple of hours to forget, be happy and to focus on something else other than the escalating Tsunami that she was embroiled in. Esther was able to enjoy and remind herself during every session how very content and thankful she was.

> Unconscious behaviour means that we are not fully conscious, or aware, of what we are doing.
>
> Source: Quora.com

> There comes a time when silence is a betrayal
> Martin Luther King Jr

Esther arrived, and as she entered the room, she immediately noticed the cease in the discussion, within the group of women already in attendance. She had noticed it before but ignored it. After giving an awkward greeting and kissing the air with a standoff hug, they settled until the session's organisers arrived.

Futures Theatre

Why We Exist

Futures Theatre was established to create and produce work that puts women at the centre. Engaging with authentic female stories and developing partnerships with brilliant artists, we create theatre which ignites conversation and engenders change.

What we do

Create theatre from our perspective and with women centre stage

Engage and collaborate with female theatre-making artists

Promote women's professional opportunities in an area of theatre

Enable women to increase their potential and be the women they were born to be

Encourage conversation and debate on issues often suppressed or ignored

How We Do It

Commission and produce new writing inspired by authentic female stories for the mainstream audience

Deliver creative engagement programmes for vulnerable women

Provide specialist training for social workers who, in turn, support the marginalised women and young people we work with

The Artistic Director and Engagement Director Creative arrived, and the session began.

Esther was mindful of the previous awkwardness she had felt when she arrived, but she had learnt from situations with Him, that she was not to ignore her gut feeling but to store it in her back-memory pocket. Esther had learnt not to ignore her intuition; it had saved her from more heartache.

She had experienced this before when He had discussed her with others. She entered, and the atmosphere changed. That feeling when she knew someone had had a good 'chat about her', and not in a positive way like friends planning a surprise party. Esther knew what she was feeling. It was her warning to be careful. Her overriding instinct in this situation was to enjoy these sessions for her own sake. She only came near to feeling this good when she was in church. A close second. Her love of learning, creating, producing, engaging, promoting, increasing her potential, all these could ignite her to a much better version of herself.

His words - 'dumb', 'stupid', 'lazy', 'aggressive' with the word added to her ability as a mother, 'lazy mum'. Slowly each and every label, He had placed on her, as each session progressed, began to fall away, like snow off a hot oven. Esther knew she would never be the same. She was liking who she was becoming again. She flowed like an open river in these sessions; creative writing was like getting to know herself, as before, liking what she stood for and who she was. She always enjoyed reading in school; it helped to block out so many things. Esther was good at blocking out negative feelings.

> Guess what happens when a victim of a smear campaign tries to correct the lies spread about them by a narcissist, sociopath, or psychopath? Typically, the victim is rightfully so distraught that the attempt actually makes the situation worse. A good response? Realize that people who believe smear campaigns are not the quality of individuals we should want in our lives anyway.
> Moving on to healthier relationships is the best option.
> -Shannon Thomas – Southlakecounselling.org.

A couple of weeks later, Esther was leaving another session she had conquered. She had never written poetry, in school finding several excuses to avoid that lesson. She was now opened to try anything, pushing her out of her comfort zone. She couldn't tell her sons there was no such word as can't but limit herself with that same word. Before she would have said a straight no and refuse to participate in the lesson, by taking out her book and reading, blocking out the teacher's request. Esther had to prove to herself she could do anything and dispense with the names she was still being called. She was thriving with the skills she had learnt.

Esther was leaving this session completely focused on her next move, to teach her sons what she had learnt, gaining self-esteem in recognising her skills; they were enjoying having their mum back and had said so. Her sons would love her achievement of writing poetry, a new phenomenon and the end result, self-affirmation.

One of the ladies from the session asked to walk with her. Esther agreed but was wary as this lady lived in the complete opposite direction. The polite chat occurred, and then she said it. 'They are talking about you.' Esther knew, but it still hurt. She asked her what she had done, and the lady explained the 'unofficial leader' of the ladies just did not like Esther and was telling the others not to trust her. Esther thanked her and walked home, briskly; she didn't want to hear anymore. Esther was reluctant to return to the sessions or even the centre, deciding to remain home.

The next sessions day arrived, and Esther stayed at home watching TV. She missed the session, but she wanted to keep a low profile. She remembered He would tell her that the football parents didn't really like her, and they were just polite to her.

It was 3 pm, and the Centre co-ordinator telephoned asking how she was. Esther said fine making an excuse she was tired and promised to attend the following week. Esther decided she would return, and when she did, no one would be aware of what she knew.

Session day arrived, and Esther dressed carefully; she had made up her mind; she was not ready to leave yet. These sessions lasted a year, and she would stay a year, she was never a quitter. On arriving, Esther had to stop herself from laughing, the look on the 'unofficial leader's' face gave her immense pleasure, her mouth had dropped open. Esther took her seat. It was not lost, as the lady, who had disclosed their 'talking sessions' trying to stifle her smile. After the session, the Centre co-ordinator asked to speak to Esther. After their conversation, the previous week, she was unsure if Esther was coming back. Esther explained she just needed a break, but she was not ready to leave. Esther knew she was getting stronger; intimidation did not work on her now. What the 'unofficial leader' was not aware of was the fact that Esther had been taught by the best - Him.

> Coronation Street's Tyrone Dobbs is set to become embroiled in a shocking new domestic abuse storyline. The loveable mechanic – played by Alan Halsall – is engaged to demanding policewoman Kirsty Soames, and The Sun reports she is set to begin psychologically abusing Tyrone, culminating in a vicious, violent attack.
>
> "Kirsty will be seen attacking Tyrone, and the fallout will be how she feels terrible about it and attempts to show some remorse."
>
> Source: Coronation Street: Tyrone Dobbs To Be Abused by Girlfriend (Spoiler)
> Huffington.co.uk
> 12/03/2012

Esther was dealing with a multiple of events, so the 'unofficial leader' at the centre was now on the back burner and was dealt with it by ignoring Her completely.

She had to concentrate on His next move: they attended court and in His papers was a letter showing He had attended an appointment at the Wandsworth Domestic Violence Centre, He was a victim of domestic abuse, His evidence was building. Esther looked at the date of 2014. She had refused to have any contact with Him since 2012; she was too busy looking after her mother. His planning was immaculate and detailed, and He always informed her exactly what His plans were, but she just didn't connect the dots.

He had told her that His family referred to Esther as 'Kirsty.' Esther was puzzled, not being familiar with the storylines of the Soaps or their characters. He watched them and reality shows as faithfully as singing His songs to her - EastEnders, Coronation Street, Big Brother, Love Island, Hollyoaks - refusing to move to deal with the children if they were on the TV. His forward planning was now coming into action.

> ### Letter to get evidence of domestic violence
>
> You need to provide 1 piece of written evidence of domestic violence to get legal aid in divorce or separation. You can use any of these sample letters to ask for proof.
>
> Source: Sample Letter to get evidence of domestic violence – Gov.uk

Esther attended the Refuge centre, asking the Centre Co-ordinator how He had obtained a letter from a domestic violence centre. She replied all are welcomed, women, children, and men. They have to be listened to, and they cannot say if the information they give is correct or not. Each centre is different regarding providing a letter to confirm they visited a centre; the length of contact is not always stated.

Esther was now at the end of the creative writing course, it was a year, time for each person to give individual positive feedback, to the group, Esther knew what was coming from Her.

'I didn't really like you at first, but over time I got to know you, and you're actually okay.'

Esther could feel the whole room go still and look at her to react.

Esther looked at Her. *'I knew you didn't really like me, but that's okay if you don't now. I'm fine with that. I like me.'*

She did not understand, Esther had been taught by an expert on trying to make her dislike herself, and she had no intention to let that happen again. Remembering her mother's quote, 'The cornerstone that the master-builder refuses.' She made no reply, and after the uncomfortable moment lapsed into silence, the Creative Co-ordinator moved the session on for others to relay their positive feedback.

The lady that had originally confirmed to Esther of certain members' discussion regarding her, now smiled at her during the session and congratulated her afterwards. Esther thanked her for telling her in the first place. Esther never thought she would meet someone like 'Him' in a group that supported victims of abuse.

Esther did not attend much of the sessions, after this day, only the sessions that interested her, as she was coming to the realisation that she needed to attend less, this season was concluding. There were now new people attending and Esther felt it was time to make way for their needs.

'Unofficial leader' stopped attending very soon after that session, after She was confronted by another client for accusing that person of 'leaking' sensitive information. She also stopped talking to all the ladies She once sat with, holding 'High tea' at their café chats.

For instance, Tina Turner in 1975 refused to change her last name after establishing herself, career-wise, with the last name of her husband and keeping it after 13 years of marriage made a lot of sense.

Children – Children are perhaps the main reason why any mother will maintain the last name after divorce.

Source: Reasons to Not Change Your Married Name After Divorce.
by Tyrone Jones
marriagenamechange.com

> If you are Black, Asian or minority ethnic women trying to escape from domestic abuse, your experience may be compounded by racism, which is pervasive in the UK.
>
> Source: Women from Black, Asian, and ethnic minority communities.
> www.womensaid.org
> Article taken for The Survivors Handbook.

Esther noted in His court documents He had changed her name, double barrelling it, by adding her maiden name. Also noted, her origin of birth was in Jamaica. Esther was extremely proud of the place her parents were born; however, she only knew England as her birthplace. She did not think it was important until she arrived at the Cafcass office, and they refused to give her a copy of the court prepared report. They informed her that her ID, passport, did not match the name they have from the court. Esther explained once she married, she had changed to His name and had used that name for the past 7/8 years, producing her passport, as her ID.

The receptionist explained she would have to discuss this with her manager. After waiting 15 minutes, the receptionist returns with the report and a document for Esther to sign, taking note of her passport details as evidence, which was then returned to her.

Esther now realised that this could possibly be an ongoing difficultly and immediately attended the Refuge centre for advice. Her usual support worker was not present, so she spoke to the person on duty, explaining the problem she was having with her ID and that He had changed her name.

The person on duty bluntly told her *"In my experience, I have not heard of a perpetrator changing a victim's name on forms or their place of birth.'* Esther felt deflated. It had just made a huge difference to her, whilst at the Cafcass office this morning. The old Esther, a year ago, would have just walked away and not responded, but she could hear her voice say. *'But you would not have any idea how I, as a black woman, would feel with my name and place of birth changed and having to prove who I am'.*

The person on duty still saw this as not an issue and could help no further or give any suggestions on how to resolve this matter, turning away to her desk. Esther saw this as an indication to leave. Esther discussed this with the Centre Manager when she returned. She listened to Esther and agreed to raise this in the next client meeting to look at as another form of abuse - a perpetrator may use – changing a victim's identity on court documents. The Centre Manager agreed the type of abuse could change direction at any time.

The court date arrived, and the magistrates asked his reasons for changing Esther's name to a double-barrelled surname. He felt that she should not have dropped her maiden name when they married. He further explained He felt that she should have kept both names and now was the time to give her back her maiden name. The order was clear, Esther was to be referred to by her married name, especially as this was upsetting their children to see the letters arriving with the change of Esther's surname.

He ignored the order, and when He addressed her formally in emails would double-barrel her name. When the divorce came through many years later, He only referred to Esther by her maiden name.

> I'm getting divorced, but I'm not divorcing my son, he's a Hollywood. I'm his mum and, I'm not going to get rid of his name.
>
> Alex Hollywood, The Chef

Esther watched Alex Hollywood's interview as she was asked the question if she would be keeping the name of her ex-husband and on hearing her explanation, on Loose Women, Esther stood up and clapped. How very well said for all the women who have to justify keeping their ex-husband's name.

Affirmation of Princes

I am a place of care, kindness and discretion
I am inspirational
I am a beautiful feeling of awesomeness
I am smart, helpful and respectful
I am lifted high by God
I am in a happy place
I am a king
I am smiling all the time
I am fun and laughter
I am amazing

Elaine Duffus 17/05/2016

8th Campaign - **Mediation - Cafcass**

> Mediation is a procedure in which the parties discuss their disputes with the assistance of a trained, impartial third person who assists them in reaching a settlement.
>
> The term "mediation" broadly refers to any instance in which a third party helps others reach an agreement. More specifically, mediation has a structure, timetable, and dynamics that "ordinary" negotiation lacks. The process is private and confidential, possibly enforced by law.
>
> Source: Wikipedia.org
>
> If mediation doesn't work or is not appropriate, we will issue a C100 to indicate you have attended mediation or a mediation information assessment meeting (MIAM). This is a form you will need if you wish to apply to court for a court order
>
> Source: Family Matters Mediation.co.uk

He and Esther had attended several Mediation services, over the years, two arranged by Esther, unsuccessfully. When Esther received a letter to attend Mediation that He had arranged, she was dubious, but she thought maybe just maybe they could resolve the arrangements for the children. There were planned arrival and departure times to the venue they were meeting at, to avoid contact. The sessions were conducted with each in separate rooms, and after a couple of sessions, it was agreed by both, this could now be moved to being in the same room. He arrived and began to take notes.

Esther asked if that was allowed as the meeting was a confidential meeting. She could see He was annoyed as He packed His note pad away. *'Always on duty'* she thought.

The first meeting went well setting up the childcare arrangements. At the second session with them both in the room, the discussion concluded He had not kept to the schedule He had agreed. Esther was silent as she knew to venture into this discussion; she would be the target. He saw no reason to leave her out and transferred His attention to her with the name calling beginning, *"You're lazy."* Esther knew it was coming, but He always kept it in check when others were around. She asked If she could leave, waiting for their permission. She knew she wasn't returning back to that room. They had 2 Mediators in the session, male and female, and the female mediator followed to the door, asking if she was okay. Esther assured her that she was.

When the court date arrived, Esther contacted mediation and asked if they could write a letter saying it was not her fault that mediation sessions had failed. It was at this stage she was informed that their confidentiality policy included all events, including abusive interaction, that occurred during mediations. These could not be relayed to the courts. His plan to take this to court had succeeded.

Children And Family Court Advisory and Support Service

Cafcass looks after the interest of the children involved in family proceedings. It is independent of the courts and social services but works under the rules of the Family Court and legal to work with children and their families, and then advise the courts on what is considered to be the best interest of individual children.

Source: www.cafcass.gov.uk

Each time Esther received a letter using the double-barrelled name, she knew she was being summoned to court, with His allegations the Child Arrangement order had been breached. Each court appearance a different Cafcass officer was allocated, to represent the children's views.

> Domestic violence has been shown to affect the Black community disproportionately – Black women experience domestic violence at rates 30 or 50 per cent higher the white women.
>
> "In many cases, we don't ask for help because we have internalized this idea, we need to be strong," says Flowers. "This idea of strong Black women is rewarded and is something that can even be a source of resilience. But it can also leave us feeling like we have no one to turn to."
>
> Source: Black Women are staying Silent Why some Black Women feel like they can't disclose domestic violence by Amanda Kippet Apr 09, 2018.

The first Cafcass officer, a black woman, called Esther to request that the children arrive at the offices in Croydon and Esther to bring someone to watch the children, while she was being interviewed. Esther asked her niece to attend.

The children were interviewed first. 'The baby' who was now aged 4, went in and came out almost immediately, with no hesitation he wanted to see his father and was excited if this could happen. Their older son stayed longer, in the meeting room, he had stated from the offset he wanted no contact with his father, which he had been saying for several years and even wanted to change his name, made more compelling with his father changing Esther's married name. James informed the first Cafcass officer of all his concerns and even wrote a letter to the judge, why he shouldn't go.

Esther's interview was relaxed, and she felt it had gone well. As He had taken her to court, He was interviewed beforehand. He had said she was a good mum and that He just wanted to see His sons. Esther agreed, but she wanted no contact with Him. The Cafcass Officer asked if there was a reason. *'I just think it's best'* Esther replied, not feeling comfortable to tell the true reason.

How would this strong black woman see her if she had told her the truth? Would she even believe her? He came across so charismatic and charming, always protesting He was the victim.

> Triangulation consists of bringing the presence of another person into the dynamic of the relationship, whether it be an ex-lover, a current mistress, a relative, or a complete stranger.
>
> Source: Taken from bestselling book Psychopath Free by Jackson Mackenzie. Noted in Article 5 Forms of Narcissistic Abuse That Narcissists Use To Get Inside Your Head Written Shahida Arabi |Self|April 22, 2020.

In the past, He would gloat how women thought she was so lucky to have such an attentive and good husband. He would point out loads of women He thought were looking at Him. When she made it clear she wanted to end the marriage, this was His go to quote, *"There's lots of women that would want me, and I could be with anyone."*

He had tried to make her jealous of a mother at their son's sporting activity. It came to a head when Esther told one of the coaches what He was saying. The coach arranged a meeting with a few parents, and it was revealed He was discussing their issues with this mother and was using this situation to say she liked Him. She strongly denied this and did not want to be drawn into a dispute.

As Esther, her children and her niece were on their way to the lifts, to leave the Cafcass building, when the Cafcass officer asked to have a quick word. Esther moved a little distance away from the children and her niece. The Cafcass officer lowered her voice, , *'Next time you attend any meetings with the children, please do their hair.'* Esther stepped back; all her sons had long hair that was cornrowed, hanging down to their shoulders. She knew their hair was neat and tidy, brushing their hair every morning. Esther left the office asking her niece how she felt the boy's hair looked, 'Lovely', her niece replied.

Esther asked James several times to reconsider going to watch his brother, who was still quite young to be away from home and he would be able to help with his younger brother's asthma and eczema medication. James refused.

What the court will decide?

The court will make the final decision about what should happen to your children after reading the Cafcass workers report and listening to what you and other people in the case have said.

The court will:
- Pay particular attention to your children's wishes and feelings but may not always do what your children want
- Make its decision based on what it thinks is best for your children
- Set its decision out in 'court order' which you must stick to.

If you are not happy with the court's decision, you must raise this at court – you cannot make a complaint to us about the court's decision.

Source: Cafcass.gov.uk

The section 7 report read as followed - The children are to have staggered contact/ contact is to be built up to regain a relationship with their father – starting with a day contact and building to overnight stays. Esther began preparing the boys for their weekend contact.

This investigation is known as a Section 7 Report. The Report will take around 12 weeks to be completed. During this time, if necessary, extra information can be obtained from the police, doctors, schools, children's services, or any other appropriate person involved with the family.

Source: Children Act 1989| Cafcass – Jordans Solicitors
www.jordanssolictors.co.uk

The Court date arrived, with the Section 7 report making little effect. The judge saw no reason why the boys should not immediately begin overnight stays with their father. The first Cafcass officer was not at court to discuss or interject her response. Esther knew James would be distraught.

He was over the moon. He had won and was punching the air in delight.

Esther left the courtroom going immediately to the boys who were in the contact suite, on the top floor of Holborn court.

'But they didn't listen. I don't want to go. The judge did not read my letter. He knows I don't like sleepovers' He was crying uncontrollably. Esther had not even thought of this. Her son was right, and he had never liked to be away from her from since he was very little, even refusing to attend sleepovers at his Godmothers home, unless Esther attended.

Esther reassured their son, he would have a great time at his grandparents, seeing his beloved grandfather. She even explained she needed the rest, with His dad now going to take him to his sporting activities. James looked horrified and cried even louder. There was nothing she could say or do, and the courts had decided they had to start their contact straight away, meeting their father and start overnight contact the following weekend.

James cried all the way home, and once home there was no consoling him, he did not want to attend, refusing to eat or sleep, crying most of the evening until he fell asleep.

> Custodial parents face a difficult issue when a minor child refuses to visit the other parent. This refusal may result from Alienation, anger, and sometimes fear. The situation is increasingly problematic as the child approaches the age of majority (18 years old)
>
> Sometimes it depends on which judge is hearing the matter.
>
> On the one hand, the custodial parent doesn't want to face penalties or possible jail time for violating a court-imposed custody schedule. The custodial parent's attorney has a duty to help the client avoid these situations. But on the other hand, the custodial parent naturally wants to protect the child from potential psychological or physical trauma resulting from forcing the child to visit an untrustworthy parent.
>
> Source: Sections used - Avoiding Contempt When
A Child Refuses to Visit with a Parent.
www.cooleyhandy.com

The fortnightly weekend contact began, with James continually protesting as each visit drew near, not wanting to attend. Esther continued encouraging him, using the responsibilities that he needed to help look after his younger brother and her need to rest at the weekends. The boys had never been separated for long periods of time, even a couple of days had seen them both yearning for the company of the other. The protests would increase to see each other after a period of long separation. Eventually, Esther said to him *"Well, it cannot be that bad."* James just replied, *"You don't understand; I just don't want to go."*

James attended a couple of weekend contact but was making his own plans, reading the Rights of the Child, and then executed his plan, booking himself into the Afterschool club. His father arrived to collect him, and his younger brother, as per court order and James refused to leave the building. There was nothing He or the Head Teacher could do, James would not budge. He left with their younger son, extremely angry, of course, it was her fault. She had 'brainwashed' their son to not attend weekend contact.

Esther was totally unaware contact had not occurred and was settling down for a quiet weekend, when the telephone call came through from the school, asking her to collect James. Esther cried all the way to collect James from school, knowing they would have to return back to court, and she feared she would be blamed, and the consequences to follow. There was no way James was going back, his stubborn streak had kicked in, and he wasn't listening to her, which was very unusual. Something had happened.

A new court date arrived, He had brought the matter back to court, as Esther had feared, with the main point listed as Parent Alienation. James was still refusing to attend weekend contact and refusing to give his reasons.

Esther was driving to collect James from his activity, with her younger son in the back seat, both singing along to the songs on the radio.

'Mum, James told dad he wasn't coming back, and they had a big argument.' Esther listened; her younger son had kept it until it was just the two of them.

"Daddy was rude to James and said he has to come because of the court order and James said he's not coming back. And James was upset and said he didn't care about the court order. James said he wasn't coming back. Daddy said he had to." Esther asked who else was there. "Everyone" he replied. Esther was sad no one intervened.

This was the child who due to his small size they all called 'little man'. He had arrived several weeks earlier, so his physical development was slow. He was the child even she had underestimated. He was quiet when anything happened but had the ability to absorb everything and more importantly recite exactly to the letter and word how events occurred. On meeting her younger son, people immediately thought he was much younger until he spoke. His tiny stature was not a reflection of his age and his intelligence. He was the spokesperson for his brother. The matter returning to court saw the allocation to a different Cafcass Officer, and now additional services were also allocated to the case, mediation for James and attending Separated Parenting Program, all compulsory, for both of them. He had already attended a course, and he proudly informed the courts.

> The Separated Parents Information Programme (SPIP) is a course which helps you understand how to put your children first while you are separating, even though you may be in dispute with your child's other parent. The course helps parents learn the fundamental principles of how to manage conflict and difficulties.
>
> You will not attend the same session as your ex-partner. In some areas, it is free to attend – you can contact your local provider for more information.
>
> Being ordered to attend by the court
>
> Courts have the power by making an order, to 'direct' parents to attend a programme aimed at promoting safe contact with children. Cafcass is usually asked to advise the court if it is suitable for you. You can be ordered to go to a SPIP (these is no charge for Cafcass service user to attend) and/or to a Mediation Information and Assessment Meeting (MAIM)
>
> Source:Cafcass.gov.uk

He was actually proud of attending this course as a mature parent. Esther felt it was shameful and disrespectful.

Esther's initial response was why did she, aged 40+, have to attend a parenting class? She wasn't sure if she should be vexed or insulted. Parenting class for a mother that was parenting 3 children, 2 under the age of 10 and her oldest son with additional needs. She had to talk to someone.

Lorna listened to Esther's strong arguments against attending and calmly pointed out and agreed, yes it was it was an insult, but however she had no choice as the court had instructed this and all they were seeing were two parents not agreeing on contact. Esther protested at the unfairness of her having to attend. Lorna moved on to outline the benefits of attending this course. Lorna reminded Esther that she had to go back to her own philosophy, each part of this process was a learning curve, and she should never question her parenting skills and more importantly, herself.

Esther arrived first on this course, with the room gradually filled with other parents, with a few reluctant participants. There were all handed a work booklet, with sections to be completed, as they advanced through the session. The front cover was of a young child standing, covering their ears as the partial image of their parents was in the background, obviously disagreeing. Esther felt in the pit of her stomach churn; she was justified in her thoughts. They believed they were in dispute over the children. She 100% wanted Him to see the children; she just did not want to have anything to do with Him.

The course was well structured, with 9 men and 1 woman in attendance. Esther felt unsettled; she could feel the anger in the room, especially from some fathers. Esther was the only black woman on the course.

However, there was one white father, who stood out to her; he had a softly spoken manner, was the sole carer for his children. He articulately described his wishes regarding the wellbeing and paramount needs of his children.

Esther related so much to this parent. He did not want the constant battling, explaining he and his partner had separated, and due to her ongoing medical issues, he was granted the care of their children. He saw no reasons for his ex-partner not to have 100% access to their children; however, the children needed consistency and structure. Outlining everything Esther was against: children being taken and not returned back on time, and on some occasions not knowing when they would return home, eating whatever they wanted – even if it was against their medical needs, with him having to deal with the consequences of this – allergies and eczema.

They were both ordered by the court and placed on this program, even though he had complied with the Child Arrangement Order. He was hoping that this would be the final time they had to go back to court, as with them both attending there could be some resolution towards children's needs coming first.

Esther's confirmation was received; something positive had to come out of this.

His final words sent a gasp around the room from other parents, including Esther - He had been attending court for 7 years. He hurriedly explained, "on and off." He hoped it would be the final time. He sounded so hopeful and optimistic, Esther hoped and prayed this would be the case.

Esther had been to court now for over a year. His returning this matter back to court, He was hoping the courts would instruct James to attend contact visits. Esther could not imagine being in court for 2 years much less 7 years!

Esther admired this man's strength and his serene way of explaining his situation, but more importantly, whenever a disgruntled father became hostile, he would step in, with his quiet manner and remind them that the children were the paramount concern. His manner was like cool water over a burning fire.

He was a parent whose sole priority was the care of his children, not to be bankrupt with court fees. He was an engineer, on a good salary; however this was having an affect on his finances – court fees, Solicitors and Barrister costs, time off work, paying childcare costs when he was at court or on this course, school fees. His sadness came with his children constantly going to court over this period and the emotional impact on them.

Esther left that course knowing she had no choice but to talk her truth, feeling like 'The drop that made the vase overflow.' She was the vase that had received her drop.

> The Family Mediation Council's Code of Practice requires that all children and young people aged 10 and above should be offered the opportunity to have their voices heard directly during the Mediation if they wish.
>
> Source: Family Mediation Council.org.uk

Returning to court not only saw the change of a Cafcass Officer to the case but being assigned before a new bench of magistrates. They were unwilling to demand James attend contact and wanted him to attend mediation to discuss the reason for his refusal. This was totally unexpected, Esther anticipated she would be blamed and even fined for not making their son attend contact.

Esther attended the exact location, she had attended for the Separated Parents Program, for mediation meeting with the manager of the centre. The assessment was completed, and Esther explained she was not at fault if their son refused to attend the sessions. The Manger snapped back *'They were not here to take sides.'* Esther fell silent; this was unexpected. The Manager continued by explaining the schedule of meetings. Esther was to attend and meet with the Cafcass Family Court Advisor, who would then meet James. There would then be a meeting with James and his father, over a period of 3-4 meetings, depending on how the first meeting went.

Esther returned and explained the plan to James, who was still refusing to attend, seeing no need to meet with his father. Esther thought it was pointless to pursue this now, she would address this again when the appointment letter arrived, and she would also mention this to his mentor.

> ### Domestic abuse
>
> Our primary role in every case we're involved with is to safeguard the child and ensure that their best interest are presented within the court proceedings. Domestic abuse is a concern in a significant proportion of our private law (divorce and separation) cases. It is our role to assist the court to carefully balance their decision so that the children and adults are kept safe and that children are able to maintain a relationship with both parents where this is safe and in their best interest.
>
> Source: Cafcass.gov.uk

The second Cafcass worker was a Caucasian lady, with a no-nonsense approach, who Esther thought was just unpleasant. Her manner, when speaking to Esther, was blunt and cutting. She could not understand why they *'Just could not sort it out between them with the child arrangements and them both be reasonable.'* She was reluctant to meet with the boys, in person. She wanted to conduct interviews by telephone, seeing they didn't need to attend the Cafcass office again.

Esther was advised to not disagree with her and attended the office to meet with her. She was also due to attend the children's school to meet with them and also speak to their Head Teacher. This time Esther decided to bring evidence. The Cafcass officer took the bundle of paperwork that Esther gave her, placing them on a table beside her, not opening them and said she would review them later and let her know. The meeting was blunt and to the point. The children's needs were paramount, and Esther and their father were to put their differences aside and work together. Esther remains to her stance – He could have access to the children not her. The Cafcass Officer was not happy with her response. She called before the court date to say she had reviewed the paperwork and did not feel it was necessary to include them, giving her reasons that Esther had not presented this information in the first hearing. She was just giving it now to *'win points.'*

The words *'Don't disagree with the Cafcass officer it could go against you'* still rang in Esther's mind and she fell silent, she was not believed. She asked Esther to collect the copies of possible evidence - photographs, notes, and texts, of abuse. Esther declined and advised her to destroy them as she felt fit. She advised Esther they would be destroyed, and Esther replied in a monotone voice *'fine.'*

UK Mediation

Ethical Practice for Mediators
Empathy-Integrity-Competence- Fairness – Non-Maleficence.
Source: www.ukmediation.net

Children will be given a greater voice in the family justice system so they can tell the judges how they feel and what they think about the family disputes they are involved in.

The government will also work with mediator sector so that children have appropriate access to mediators in cases which affect them.

Source: www.gov.uk

James was refusing to attend mediation, even with Esther giving him unrelenting reminders that he needed to at least attend the session to give his reasons. James was attending his mentor sessions, and Esther, who usually sat in the reception area, was asked to attend also. The mentor felt that Esther was placing a lot of pressure on James to attend mediation, and he should be allowed to attend on his own free will. Esther explained to his mentor that the court order stated the need for James to attend mediation, and she would be in contempt of court if he did not attend. The mentor explained the courts understand when children do not attend mediation and Esther's constant reminders, he needed to attend was causing James unnecessary stress, and he was already feeling the pressure of the court procedure.

Esther and James both expressed their fears, Esther; being in contempt of court and James; meeting with his father. The mentor asked Esther not to discuss with James the court proceedings; however, they will continue to discuss, in depth, James fears, in their sessions. James and Esther agreed.

James eventually decided to attend mediation. The letter arrived, and he attended the first assessment meeting and then it was agreed the next meeting would be with his father.

James woke early, unable to eat, saying he was nervous and scared. How would he tell his father he didn't ever want to see him again? They travelled by bus in silence. Esther couldn't think of anything to say, and James remained in his own silence. Theirs was a relationship that didn't need words; they were at ease with each other.

They arrived at the contact centre, and Esther was asked to return in 2 hours. Esther avoided eye contact with James, his eyes always told her how he felt, and if she looked in his eyes, she would have been reluctant to leave him. She said her goodbyes, forcing herself to sound as cheerful as possible, leaving the building and began walking towards Lewisham shopping centre.

Esther wandered, avoiding looking at anything or anyone, just walking. She did not have any money to go shopping, even though the boys were in desperate needs of bits and pieces, but the ongoing court procedure was again leaving her unable to provide the things they needed, with her having to save for a length of time before she could purchase them. Every purchase had to be planned to the penny.

After 30 minutes or so, Esther decided to call a friend, Louretta, placing herself at a nearby bus stop, from the contact centre. Unexpectedly, the call from the contact centre came through 15 minutes into her telephone conversation, Esther hurriedly ended her call. She needed to return back as the contact had ended and He had left the building 10 minutes earlier. Esther arrived and was led into the back room. James was seated, she could tell by his eyes he had become distressed, and she resisted hugging him.

The Contact Supervisor explained that James had met with his father.

After 30 – 40 minutes, James had become upset and asked to have a break and then refused to enter the room again. His father was then asked to leave. They also did not feel it necessary to book further meeting as James had informed them, he would not be returning for any further meetings. Esther asked if that was allowed, as the court had asked for 2-3 meetings. The Contact Supervisor says she would pass James' reluctance on to Cafcass to feed back to the court. Esther nodded in agreement, looking at James. As if on cue, James responded.

'He does not listen to me.'

Esther immediately knew what had happened.

At court, the mediation report was read out by the Cafcass Officer, who was in attendance. All professionals felt it would be unfair to force James to attend further mediation or contact with his father. His McKenzie expressed His views. He felt that Esther had 'coached' James before their meeting, as these were not the words a 10-year-old would use.

The mentor had called Esther that morning, asking if she wanted to support at court, Esther eagerly agreed, not knowing how vital their attendance would be. The mentor confirmed to Esther's Barrister that James had prepared his own words and questions for his meeting, with his father. She further added that the words James used were exactly what would be expected of a child that had an articulate mother and who had received an independent school education. James was most definitely expected to express himself in this manner.

Section 7 report felt that both parents needed to look at the needs of James. Esther was dazed but not surprised, of course, she would be tarnished as being a part of the problem. The courts were reluctant to make an order forcing James to attend contact; however, If he ever at any time wished to see his father, then Esther was to facilitate this. Esther agreed.

He cried uncontrollably in court holding onto His McKenzie's forearm.

Esther felt sorry for Him, and a week later the emails arrived, full of accusations, It was her fault, and she had done this to keep more of the Child Maintenance He paid.

> **About Ransom Fonts**
>
> It takes its name from the appearance of a stereotypical ransom note, with the message formed from words or letters cut randomly from a magazine or newspaper in order to avoid using recognisable handwriting. Ransom note fonts are created to stimulate letters used in ransom notes you might see in old TV shows and films.
>
> Source: www.fontmeme.com

Esther ignored His accusations, but the last statement stood out. *'Sending any more letters.'*

A series of vile letters had begun to arrive at His selected family members, accusing one in-law of being in an alleged 'entanglement' outside his marriage. He had informed Esther of the letter, one arriving at their home, by showing it to her. The letter was neither handwritten nor typed, and the person had used the letters from a newspaper, cutting out each letter, sticking them into sentences, which formed the structure of the letter. He pointed out the postcode, across London. They reminded her of an Agatha Christie ransom note. To sit, cut out each letter and stick this together and drive across London to post, was someone that had a motive to disrupt His family member's marriage and who had a lot of time on their hands. Something Esther did not have with looking after her mother and her children. He openly accused her of doing this once their marriage was over and even though Esther had strongly denied it, even asking Him to collect all the letters and go to the Police Station to find out who had done this. He refused, saying He saw no need, as He knew it was her. Esther knew this was the final thing for His family to believe it was her. She had ended her already strained relationship with them years ago. The children attended all their family functions with Him, but she never did.

> ## Scale and pattern of returns
>
> - Of the 40,599 applications received in 2016-2017, 30% were returned, meaning at least one previous application had been made in respect of the eldest child.
> - The majority of returns involved just one previous case, but just under one-third of returns had two or more previous cases. One child had been subject in eleven cases between 2005 and 2017.
> - 63% of returns involved an application made within two years of the previous case being closed to Cafcass. Cases that had returned to court more times had a higher proportion which returned within two years
>
> Source: Private law cases that return to court: a Cafcass study by E. Halliday
> www.cafcass.gov.uk

Several years had passed, the start of Him increasingly breaching the Child Arrangement order was Esther's indication that a return to the court was inevitable. His reason remained the same - Parental Alienation - to re-establish contact with James and increase contact times for their younger son, who was now 9 years old.

There was now an allocation of a third Cafcass Officer, who they met on the actual court date. She met with the boys first and then called Esther for her interview. The Cafcass officer explained she had telephoned several times to talk to Esther before the court date and was unable to make contact. Esther was unsure but asked the question regardless, *'Who gave you my number?'* The Cafcass worker seemed unsure how to reply, *'Not to worry'*, and began her interview.

The questions began - Did she feel He should have more time with the younger son? Esther agreed with His request. Regarding James, Esther had no control; he was an independent traveller; he could now attend at any time if he wished. Esther wanted very limited contact with Him and as the boys grew older felt this was now possible to maintain their distance. Cafcass Officer agreed with the views of the boys and their explanation of the situation around contact; it was best that He had limited contact with Esther also. She complimented Esther on how both boys were well-mannered and able to vocalize their wishes with clarity. She was equally surprised and impressed with James' adamant attitude to attend school as soon as he was spoken to, wanting to complete his subject assessments, especially as some children did not like doing tests and would have used attending court to miss school tests altogether. Esther thanked her and explained he was committed to his education.

Their younger son asked only to attend once a month; this was a huge shift from the original Child Arrangement order. Esther informed the Cafcass Officer she was aware of both boy's views, but if He wanted to keep their youngest until Monday, taking him to school, she was fine with this; agreeing this might lessen the conflict at contact times.

The Cafcass Officer was a small caucasian woman and very quietly spoken. She did not inquire about the reason for the youngest son now wanting to reduce contact. It was as if it was the parental conflict was seen as the reason for his reluctance to attend.

Her belief appeared to be that to reduce contact with Esther would cause everything to then settle into a more relaxed pattern. She counted out the dates of contact with Esther, as He would now be taking their son to school Monday mornings.

Esther wanted to cry; they still did not get it, hoping things would change, with this now moving to at most 7 contacts for the year; it must work, right?

Esther thought they never ask children the right questions, and yes, we live in hope for change.

> **Abusive men using child contact as a way to carry on subjecting women to domestic abuse**
>
> Women are being subjected to coercive control and physical and even sexual assault from their ex-partners when children are being picked up or dropped off. Campaigners say abusers also carry on terrorising their victims during child custody battles in the family courts and harassing them via email, reportedly the problem is getting worse.
>
> Julian Watkins, senior research analyst at Safe Lives, said: "We started collecting data on this issue over the last couple of years because domestic violence services and the survivors they support were increasingly telling us it is a problem."
>
> The domestic abuse charity has found abusive former partners use childcare arrangements to carry on targeting their victims in around a third of cases where children were cited as the reason for ongoing contact.
>
> Parents face fines or even jail sentences if they do not make sure their child sees an ex-partner on a supervised or unsupervised visit court-ordered is in place.
>
> Source: The Independent, Maya Oppenheim Women's correspondent Sunday 13 October 2019 17.34

Esther was fearful. He would not like the boy's views. He would blame her, and she would be later punished by His email, returning to the courtroom to present findings before the magistrates.

The magistrates asked that the children's views be presented first. The Cafcass officer presented the boys' views - James wanted the arrangements to remain the same, no contact. Their youngest son was the most expressive – telling of the disturbances at contact times, verbal abuse to his mother, his father not staying in the allocated area when he was returned home, returning home late sometimes in the dark, Him not *'sticking to any rules.'* It began with a few grunts, coming from Him, with the magistrate asking if He had anything to say. He replied bluntly, *'No.'* Listening to the Cafcass Officer final request - their youngest son wanted only to attend once a month.

He became emotional, sniffing at first, with one of the magistrates asking if he was okay, did He need some water or time outside. He refused. Esther's mind ran to *'Crocodile tears'*, She had seen this before, the tears in public then the private storm of accusations.

His McKenzie friend went; next, his response abrupt, aggressive and uncensored, *"The children are despicable for saying such lies regarding their father."*

'Despicable.' Esther rolled this word over in her mind; she had tuned out the rest of His comments. He felt her children were *'Despicable'* – and His McKenzie was not referring to the cutest yellow minion we love to see in a children animation movie –

Definition – Despicable meaning very unpleasant, evil, disgusting, vile.

This was a representative of an organisation, which promoted that the children's needs must be paramount, had now resorted to calling her children names.

> Estranged fathers with an alleged or proven history of domestic abuse can use parental Alienation claims to discredit mothers and gain parenting time with their children, a new study shows.
>
> Parental Alienation (PA) is recognised by the Children and Family Court Advisory and Support Service (CAFCASS) as 'when a child's hostility towards one parent is not justified and then is the result of psychological manipulation by other parent.'
>
> A researcher at Brunel University London examined all 40 reported and published private family law judgements in England and Wales, from 2000 to 2019, in which parental alienation was raised. They found that PA has become part of a shrewd rhetoric in custody battles concerning children, including those who experience domestic abuse. These cases may be the tip of the iceberg because the vast majority of private law judgement are not published in the law reports.
>
> The research identified a pattern of abusive parents, usually the father, accusing the parent with custody of alienating the children against them. In some instances, this became grounds for transfer of residence of the child. The research also raises questions about the purpose and use of PA in private law proceedings in the family courts.
>
> Source: Playing the Parental Alienation cardAbusive parents use the system to gain access to children, by Simone McNicholas-Thomas 20 Jan 2020.

The McKenzie friend then moved on to quote His usual script - Parent Alienation statement. Esther had this uneasy feeling that never left her when she heard this PA statement. She had never heard of Parental Alienation before and she in no way expected that this would be believed.

The Cafcass officer interjected, *'The children have the utmost exceptional manners and were extremely articulate.'* Further explaining, she did not believe the children were lying or were being 'coached' before the court dates.

The court order that James was to have no contact, if he changed his mind, Esther was to facilitate contact. The youngest son would increase his contact time with his father.

Their youngest son was informed, and his immediate response was, *'I knew they wouldn't listen to me. What's the point?'* Esther assured him that he would have the best time at his dads, and contact would be settled. In her heart, Esther didn't believe this, but she hoped, always hopeful everything would settle.

The weekend being a hassle-free zone, meaning Esther could relax and prepare for the term-time and Summer holiday assault.

The Child Arrangement Order had changed, with Esther surrendering to His requests, knowing their youngest son was unhappy. She continued persuading their youngest son it would improve, hoping that contact would settle to a simple, uneventful routine. Esther was wrong. The escalation of conflicts, was incredible, far exceeding what she had experienced in the past 6+ years.

What is DV in the military?

Domestic abuse is used in the military as a broader term that includes all forms of relationship violence against a current or former spouse or intimate partner, including physical harm and non-physical harm, like harassment and emotional abuse.

Source: www.womenslaw.org

He continued as before, His campaign not missing a beat, as if the court date and changes to the Child arrangement order never existed and had not just occurred months before – attempting to change the contact weekends, changed dates/times when returning their youngest son at the end of the contact, turning up at the school when it was her contact.

He treated the Child Arrangement Order with contempt and was non-compliant, as if to provoke Esther into returning the matter back to court.

Nothing can dim the light that shines from within.

~ Maya Angelou

9th Campaign
Children and Family Services

> Merlin is a database run by the Metropolitan Police that stores information on children who become known to the police for any reason, this can range from being a victim of bullying to being present whilst a property is searched, this may be with a warrant or under the Police and Criminal Evidence Act, it also holds data for missing persons. They can be of any age. Entries on the database can be accessed by police officers and civilian workers.
>
> Source: Wikipedia Merlin (Database)

Esther realised, for each police report He created, an individual Merlin report is sent through to that borough's Social Services Department and the area the police were contacted. He made over 30 reports, to various police stations for various reasons, not all child-related. He appeared at court with all CAD reports to use in court. Her reports, 16, were from her local police due to His ongoing breaches to Child Arrangement Order, she couldn't remember the CAD numbers, not realising their importance.

> Services have a statutory obligation to safeguard and promote the welfare of vulnerable children and adults and can provide a Social wide range of services to children and their parents, usually within their own home environment and co-ordinated by a social worker.
>
> Source: www.familylives.org.uk

Esther's contact with Social Services was the yearly reviews she attended regarding her older son with his additional needs – educational. She never envisioned that the contact would increase to the level that it had. He warned her of the consequences, she didn't believe Him and more importantly, Esther had nothing to hide.

In the early stages of the conflict, Esther was reluctant to involve them, always thinking that things would settle down. His 'concerns' and the subsequent police visits for a welfare check had borne no further actions, and Esther and the children were always wary when the intercom rang in case it was the police calling again.

The years rolled on, and her concerns for her younger child increased, she had no choice but to ask for assistance. She sought the advice of The Refuge Domestic Violence Centre, and the suggestions were that the school could make a referral to her local Children and Family Services. Esther approached her son's school to ask for help.

Esther booked an appointment to speak to the Safeguarding officer, who in turn agreed to send off a referral to Children and Family Services, to ask to support the family. Esther walked away relieved and thinking she had to get some help from somewhere, this just could not continue.

Weeks later, the letter arrived, and it informed her that there was a report of domestic abuse around the children, and both parents would be held responsible. Esther sat stunned and confused, immediately calling the Social Worker, who wrote the letter. She was indifferent. This could not continue around the children. Esther explained that they had not lived together for years, and it was around contact difficulties occurring; there was a court order, and she had attended the school asking for help. This made things even easier for the Social Worker to make her decision, *'Then you need to return this matter back to court.'* Esther explained this was not affordable and asked if her youngest could at least be referred for some emotional support. Her reply was abrupt, *'Only if the courts decided they needed support.'*

The Social Worker had noted He lived with them. Esther informed her, He did not. Esther gave His address noted at court and asked the Social Worker to send Her letter of concerns to His address. They had actually thought the conflict was in the home of the children. Esther had seen the referral form the School Safeguarding Officer had completed, and the address was different.

> A Department of Children and Families (DCF) false allegations of child abuse and/or neglect is terrifying. It is an assault on your pride, dignity, and spirits. You can be shocked, angry, and bewildered by who could levy such false allegations against you. The allegations may even come from an anonymous person, which can only add to your frustration, fright, and shame. Your self-esteem, self-worth can be severely harmed by such heinous accusations. These false allegations of child abuse reports can be filed out of spite, for revenge, or to gain leverage in custody proceedings.
>
> Source: DCF false Allegations of Child Abuse taken from article written by Kevin Seaver
> www.seaverdclawyer.com

There were attending a sporting event, and her younger son was off playing in the grounds, another child decided to help himself to the free hot drinks and accidentally spilt a hot drink on him. Her son returned and was very quiet; Esther had thought he was having an asthma attack due to his quietness. She noticed a wet patch on his shorts and asked him to come nearer to her so that she could inspect it. Once she lifted the hem of his shorts and saw his skin, her first aid training kicked into gear, with other parents also rushing to fetch water, for Esther to soothe his thigh. It was a first-degree scald, and as the skin peeled away, Esther knew this meant trouble. Esther informed Him, by email, of the accident and the action to care for the burn. He did not reply to her information email, and she knew from his silence there would be a consequence for her to pay.

Friday, He arrived to collect their youngest son for His half-term contact, still no acknowledgement or mention of her email, notifying

Him of the accident or treatment to care for their sons burn. His silence now was usually a sign that there was something unpleasant; however, she was unsure of what was to come. The weekend passed with no contact, Esther checking her emails at regular intervals, maybe too often, but this was now her habit when her youngest son was away from her.

The emails arrived, but instead of the usual statements, there was an attachment. Esther did not have access to a printer. She called her friend Louretta, panicking so much as the attachment showed it was a letter with a hospital heading, who calmed her and advised Esther to forward the email over to her. Esther began to think of all the worse things that could have happened. Whenever her youngest son was away, Esther couldn't sleep, his asthma was a huge concern even when being managed. Louretta called back, she had screenshot it, but it was too blurred and difficult to make out, but between them, they began to try to figure out her son was not admitted, and something had happened to his finger. Esther emailed Him to ask if He could send more details as the letter was blurred. No reply. She would have to wait for her son to return. The next day, Esther went to the local shop to print out the letter and noticed the details were all hers – address and mobile details. The hospital had noted Father had brought him in but not His actual name. Esther was stunned; every part of her knew this was going to be her problem.

A couple of days later, Esther's mobile rang, she was uncomfortable answering private numbers, allowing her phone to ring out and then listening to the voicemail. Previously, He had called, withholding his number, and not speaking at first then demanding to speak to the children and now it was the police that would call to make an inquiry. Esther listened to the voicemail; it was a Social Worker asking her to call back, not giving a clue for the reason for the phone call. Esther rang back the number immediately.

'Can you explain why your son has attended A&E twice this week?' Esther said she could not because he was staying at his dad; it was holiday contact for a week. The Social Worker asked about the burn.

Esther explained the accidental burn and that He was informed of the burn also. She had no contact from Him to inform her that their son had attended the hospital to check out his accidental scald. The Social Worker confirmed her younger son had stated exactly how the accident occurred, at the hospital. Esther informed the Social Worker she was fully aware their son had attended the hospital, regarding his finger; however, He had sent through was an extremely blurred hospital report. All her emails to ask on the welfare of their son was ignored. What she could identify was that the information He had given to the hospital was all her details – her address, old mobile number. He gave no details that their son was actually staying with Him for holiday contact. On the hospital form, He had given her old mobile number which she had not used for years. If the hospital had wanted to contact her for additional medical information, it would have been impossible from these details.

Esther could understand why the Social Worker would have assumed the incidents occurred whilst in Esther's care; however, Esther drew the Social Worker's attention to the inaccuracies, the Social Worker saw no reason to address this further.

The Social Worker explained her younger son had been taken to hospital the second time regarding his finger being shut in the car door. Esther asked if he was okay. The Social Worker was unsure; she was going by the hospital report; she had not made any contact with his father. It was at this point that Esther recognised her voice. This was the same Social Worker she had spoken to a couple of months before. Esther immediately reminded her they had spoken months earlier and that He would not inform her if their son was injured, even though she had sent several emails, to ask on his wellbeing. Esther ended the conversation by suggesting the Social Worker call and ask Him for more details. Esther straight away emailed Him to ask if their son was okay. He did not reply. The Social Worker never did get back to Esther to reassure how her son was. Esther had to wait for him to return home.

Esther spoke to this duty Social Worker on several occasions over the years. Although she had concerns, each time, she was advised to return the matter back to court, there was nothing they could do.

> **How do social workers approach domestic violence?**
> Louise argues that we will 'never effectively protect children if we view the prevention of harm from domestic abuse as the victim's job.' She says that the expectation of mothers to protect their child, and then to remove their child from them when they can't do this, is the 'ultimate in victim-blaming.'
>
> Source: tranparetnproject.org.uk
> By reporting team Nov 26. 2018
> Louise Tickle's Guardian Article
>
> **Early Help Assessment**
> The Early Help Assessment replacing the Common Assessment Framework (CAF), is an early assessment and planning tool to facilitate coordinated multi-agency support.
> It enables professionals to effectively identify the emerging needs of children and young people at risk of poor outcomes; it reduces duplication of assessment and improves involvement between agencies.
>
> Source: www.Achieveingfor children.org.uk

Esther felt helpless, and there seemed to be no organisation willing to take this matter back to court; She called her friend Sonia who suggested Esther call the Early Help section in the local Children and Family department.

Her youngest son was now becoming more tearful, at the slightest thing, especially before attending contact, he had attended 2 separate counselling sessions at school and was expressing the wish to remain home and not attend contact at all.

Esther called through to main switchboard and asked to be put through to the Early Help Assessment team. She was put through to duty Children and Families Services. Esther gave her details. Yes, they were aware of her case, Oct 2019, a police report came through, and they had decided that this did not need to go over to the Early Help Assessment Team and the file was closed. Esther asked what she needs to do to open her case; she was concerned regarding her youngest child. The Social Worker on duty informed her everything had to be put in writing, and then they will decide if this goes to Early Help Assessment team. Esther asked her full name. The Social Worker's reply to this question made Esther aware that this matter was going no further, *'There is only one person with my name'*, refusing to give Esther her surname. Esther ended the call knowing this would never be sent over to Early Help Assessment Team, even if she placed her concerns in writing.

Another door had closed.

> It is vital that social workers understand what an effective response to domestic abuse is. To offer the skills and knowledge required a truly holistic approach. That's why co-ordinated support from a whole range of agencies is crucial. Social workers can build strong links with other agencies and encourage better access to services for vulnerable families.
>
> Source: The role of social workers in responding effectively to domestic abuse. Back to Practice blog 29th April 2015
> www.safelives.org.uk

Esther thought back, October 2019, she was in a dimly lit car park on the phone, to the police screaming because He was at the back of Her home. Children and Families department did not think this needed to move to Early Help assessment!!! Esther thought if this was not a reason to complete an assessment, then what would be a reason?

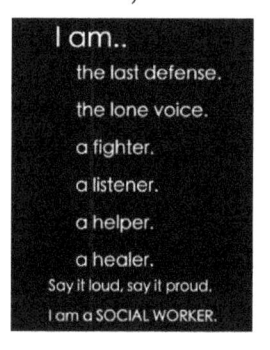

> I am..
> the last defense.
> the lone voice.
> a fighter.
> a listener.
> a helper.
> a healer.
> Say it loud, say it proud.
> I am a SOCIAL WORKER.

10th Campaign - **Medical**

Getting help and support for domestic violence

> You do not have to wait for an emergency situation to find help. If domestic abuse is happening to you, it's important to tell someone and remember that you're not alone.
> You can:
> - Talk to a doctor, health visitor or midwife.
>
> Source: getting help for domestic violence and abuse.
> www.nhs.uk

Esther had taken her youngest son out of school to attend a dentist appointment. A week later, she received a letter from the doctor informing her that He had telephoned the surgery, asking if their son had attended a doctor's appointment. The doctor had informed Him that their son had not. His email arrived that evening. *'You lied about going to the doctors.'* Esther replied they had attended a dentist due to their younger son having a toothache. He did not believe her. She didn't understand, it was her weekend contact, and she was not answerable to Him, but she did so anyway.

A few weeks later on a Sunday evening, their youngest son arrived home from weekend contact, not feeling well, complaining of a sore throat, but with no temperature. Esther emailed Him to ask for some information from the weekend. Had their son been unwell over the weekend? Had he been spitting a lot? Why was he spitting? He ignored every one of her emails. Esther sent him to school, as he said he was feeling better Monday morning and the spitting had stopped.

Her youngest son returned from school, and James noticed small rashes all over his brother's body. They rushed to the local hospital, he had Scarlet Fever. The Doctor explained this was going around the schools, and they had seen a few cases recently. He asked her youngest son how long had he been unwell? He informed the Doctor since Friday and that he was spitting a lot. The Doctor looked at Esther inquisitively. Esther informed the Doctor that he was at weekend contact with his father, and she had contacted Him; however, He had failed to reply to her email to give more information. Her son had no temperature, and she had not noticed any rashes this morning before he left for school. The Doctor informed her of the symptoms, and the only one he had complained of on his return home was the spitting and sore throat.

> Men who use coercive control against their partner, know that woman's vulnerabilities. The love and protection that many women have for their children is one area that those men use after separation to continue coercive control.
>
> Source: Using the Children www.speakoutloud.net

He continued making doctor's appointments for their youngest son, without notifying Esther, who cancelled everything else to attend. In no way did she want to be seen as a neglectful mother, by not attending their son's medical appointments. She had no idea why she was attending, and He would just send through the card at the end of weekend contact, Sunday evening. No email to explain why this would mean that Esther would also have to inform his school that their son would be absent that Monday morning.

Esther attended the 9 am appointment, with their youngest son, and on arrival was directed to see the Pharmacist. Esther has missed his asthma check, but the Pharmacist was surprised they were attending during school term, explaining they could have booked the appointment when her son was on holiday.

Esther explained that his father was making the appointments but did not inform her of the reason she was attending the surgery. She did not want to miss the appointment in case it was important. The Pharmacist agreed, and as they were here, they could have the checks done, a total of 1 hour including waiting time.

Esther was informed, He had attended to collect some of their youngest son's medication, and they had said an appointment needs to be made before the medication could be dispersed, therefore, he had made an appointment. On face value, people would think what a caring father; however, Esther knew exactly the reasons why He did not email her through the appointment details. She could have changed the appointment to a date more convenient for her son and herself. His plan was to do the complete opposite and inconvenience her, not realising it actually only caused their son to miss a lesson at school, which he would have to catch up with later.

> There are fears this lack of training means opportunities to help vulnerable abuse victims are needlessly missed.
> More than half of frontline staff say they do not feel able to identify a domestic abuse victim, according to a new survey.
>
> Source: Health staff 'missing opportunities' to spot signs of domestic abuse.
> By Sanya Burgess, news reporter

Esther telephoned to order her youngest son's asthma medication. The receptionist informed her that her son's quota of medication had been given out, and no more could be prescribed. Esther explained that it would seem high, but his father also ordered his medication.

The receptionist said, *'I understand, but no further medication could be given out.'* This conversation went on for about 15 minutes with Esther explaining she had no asthma medication for her son and why there appeared to be a high level of medication ordered. The receptionist repeated *'I do understand'*, but he could not order further prescriptions. Esther asked for the Pharmacist to please call her back, to discuss this matter urgently.

A couple of hours later, the Pharmacist called her back; the prescription was ordered and sent to the chemist to be collected later that day. Esther explained the difficulties she had in ordering the vital medication and how she had to explain everything and was still refused. The Pharmacist who was familiar with her situation advised her, in future to request her son's medication directly through her. Esther thanked her.

Esther sat at home, feeling drained. He had sent through pictures years before when they had contact on WhatsApp showing His stockpile of medications, displayed in abundance. However, when she requested their son's medication, the difficulties occurred.

Esther was finding it difficult to attend the surgery she had attended most of her life. This was the only doctor's surgery the children, and she had ever attended.

> GPs are missing vital opportunities to intervene and potentially save the lives of people experiencing domestic abuse, a leading charity has warned.
> The research, by the charity Standing Together, found that in 25% of cases, GPs failed to make inquires following disclosures or warning signs displayed by the perpetrator.
>
> Source: The Guardian Hannah Summers wed 22 Feb 2017 02.20EST.

Esther had attended the divorce proceeding and began to read His statement and evidence, handed to her in a paper bag. He had given the judge all paperwork in a folder. He had now noted she was alcohol dependent, due to her upbringing, caused by her parent's alleged continual conflict. The judge dismissed His allegations and accusations as irrelevant; this was to decide financial matters. They had attended years of child arrangements court appearances, and He had never mentioned that she had a problem with alcohol. Esther was now strong enough to tackle each and every allegation He made.

She knew exactly what she had to do; this was her reputation, so she made a Doctor's appointment and requested an alcohol and drugs test. The Doctor was reluctant and saw this as a waste of resources, as he knew the test would be negative. Esther explained the divorce proceedings and the Doctor ordered the testing, as she left the room. The Doctor said, *'I do know it's going to come back negative.'* Esther thanked him. The test arrived 2 weeks later, as predicted, it was negative. Esther asked if she could have a copy, and the doctor advised her to ask the courts to request a copy of the results from the surgery directly.

> A typical visit to the doctor for a black woman can be anything but. Stories earlier this month about Serena Williams' horrifying medical order and the high post-pregnancy mortality rates of black women show their medical concerns are often dismissed, ignored, or even chastised. Navigating this is hard enough – and even harder when the colour of your skin can mean the difference between life and death or receiving the right test to diagnose what ails you in between.
>
> Source: Doctors Don't always Believe You
> When You're a Black Woman
> by Joanne Spataro
> February 2, 3.00pm

Esther was involved in a car accident, a truck pushing her small car off the road, she attended the hospital complaining of extreme pain to her neck, back and shoulders. The hospital doctor diagnosed severe whiplash. Esther, who had never been in a car accident in her 20+ years of driving, accepted the diagnosis. The pain killers were prescribed, and the doctor also informed Esther the pain would increase but not to worry as it would subside after a while. Several visits to the hospital, her own doctors' surgery, a 6-week course of physiotherapy and Esther decided this was not whiplash. She had said this before numerous times and been ignored.

Her physiotherapist listened and felt Esther's symptoms were not progressing well; she wrote a letter requesting Esther's doctor arrange

an ultrasound appointment. This was now the third doctor that Esther had seen at her surgery, and again this doctor was also reluctant to make the appointment, looking over the physiotherapists report with suspicion. When she asked where in the report had it recommended an ultrasound, Esther pointed to the word 'ultrasound', the doctor with a not too pleased expression, reluctantly made the appointment.
In September of that year, 7 months after the accident, Esther was an ultrasound scan, at Guy's & St. Thomas' hospitals, watching as the Sonographer rolled the Transducer Probe over an area of her shoulder.

'There its is', the Sonographer said, finding what she wanted to locate. The ultrasound clearly revealed that Esther had sustained an injury to her shoulder. Esther blinked as the sonographer rolled over the area again to confirm before making notes. Esther asked her if she was sure. The Sonographer pointed to the area to show where the injury was. Esther's feelings of anger and relief washed over her. She was not lying. The pain and how her body was feeling was not in her head; the attitude shown by all the professionals she had encountered over the last 7 months had made her feel like a fraud. Like He and others had made her feel.

The buses were on diversion due to the Central London climate change march, Esther didn't feel like going on a bus, and so she began to walk home. Her thoughts were running over the past months of being made to look as though she was exaggerating her injuries which caused none of the medical or legal professionals to believe her. This now made her look at the ongoing issues with Him, she couldn't understand it, but it felt there was a similarity, again she wasn't sure why, but it was. That lingering feeling stayed with her.

> Good medical records - whether electronic or handwritten – are essential for the continuity of care of patients. Adequate medical records enable you or somebody else to reconstruct the essential parts of each patient contact without reference to memory, They should therefore be comprehensive enough to allow a colleague to carry on where you left off.
>
> The main reason for maintaining medical records is to ensure continuity of care for the patient. They may also be required for legal purposes if, for example, the patient pursues a claim following a road traffic accident or an injury at work.
>
> Source: Medical records
medicalprotection.org

Esther requested her medical file and went to the surgery to collect it. She arrived at the surgery, and the receptionist asked for her ID, she showed her passport, and the receptionist hugged Esther's file to her chest. *'Please read through your file, as there are some things you may not want to share with others.'* Esther agreed, and the receptionist handed over the file. Esther found it strange that the doctor's receptionist insisted Esther read her file and to be careful who read it also. Esther wasn't planning to read this lengthy file; however, the receptionist's actions made her now rethink this decision. The file was repetitive, Esther was going to give up, but she had an urge to read just a little further.

5th March 2015. He had called her doctors initially asking the Doctor to help her but not to tell her of His call, but to report that she was violent. The doctors were concerned about the safety of the children. He reassured the Doctor that Esther was only violent to Him and never the children. The doctor advised Him to seek legal advice to gain access to see the children.

Esther sat in her car, unable to move. He had called her Doctor and said this. Esther kept reading her medical notes. She rang her Pastor to talk and then rang her friend, Ms T. who advised what to do. Esther rang the surgery to arrange an appointment with the doctor, who had taken the call and made the notes, all those years ago.

A few days later, Esther attended the surgery, for her routine medical check-up, so this would be her opportunity to address this matter after that part of the appointment was completed. Esther was informed the appointment was for another doctor. Esther asked why this appointment was changed to another Doctor. The receptionist was unsure. Esther rearranged the appointment again, asking that the appointment had to be with this particular doctor.

14th Feb 2020, Esther entered the Doctor's examination room and underwent her routine checks, and when the Doctor asked if there was anything else, Esther saw her opportunity. She was nervous, taking a deep breath, she removed her bulky medical notes from her bag. Her heart racing and her hands shaking, Esther read, with an unsteady voice, the notes written on 5th March 2015. The Doctor listened, and Esther moved on to ask if these notes could be removed from her file. Without hesitation, the Doctor swung around on her chair to face her desk. 'I don't see why not. It's not medically related' and deleted this section of the notes. She then showed Esther the screen that this section of her notes was no longer there. Before leaving the Doctor's room, Esther left several boxes of chocolates for Valentine's day, to share with doctors and medical staff. Esther thanked the Doctor for believing her, updating her file and left the surgery. Esther never mentioned that she was the very Doctor who had made the notes.

This was her way of dealing with situations, as anything else made her seem as He had painted her. Esther was also thankful and grateful to her wise friends, always advising her - 'Good friends are better than pocket money' (No amount of money in the world could replace having true friends).

Esther had felt there was a barrier with her care highlighted when she sustained an injury from the car accident, even contemplating moving to another surgery, moving anywhere, just to get away from Him and

His accusations. Esther decided there, and then, she wasn't moving anywhere, from this surgery or this area. Why would she move from all she knew?

> Being on the receiving end of blame can be exhausting, exasperating and painful. It can make you feel tiny: like nothing you do is good enough or ever will be. It can break down your sense of trust in your partner and replace it with a growing sense of resentment and anger.
> And, if it persists for a long time, constant blame in a relationship can be a symptom of emotional abuse.
>
> Source: My partner blames me for everything
> www.relate.org.uk

Esther had heard the rumours and ignored them until her own niece confirmed, *'He did not want to have another child.'* She had a longing for another child, and they had both wanted a girl, so His statement hurt in an indescribable way. She had always had this feeling that her youngest son was seen as the reason for the breakup of their marriage, but she knew this was not true. Esther left it; she was tired of justifying His comments of untruth.

Esther's youngest son whispered the question, *'Mummy did you really want me?'* Looking into his eyes, Esther knew immediately why he had asked, without hesitation. *'With all my heart and that is why I always say I wish I had two of you because you are so special,'* hugging him so tight he screamed with laughter, calling to be released from her hug. Esther knew this was not enough to reassure her son, but for now, it was all she could do. This was her special boy, and each time she looked at him, it was like looking at her mother.

The arrival of her medical notes stunned her that He had contacted her doctor, but there was a silver lining in this dark cloud.

Esther sat with her youngest son, to explain a letter on her medical notes – for years mummy and daddy had tried for a baby and they went to a special place to have some tests. The doctors said mummy could not have any more babies and mummy and daddy cried so much.

Her son still looked confused. Esther smiled and explained, *'I prayed really hard, and God gave you to me. You are my very special baby because the doctors could not help me, but God did.'* Her son ran around the room with the letter in his hand, repeating *'I was wanted. I am the special child'*.

The letter was from a fertility clinic; they had both attended, desperate for another child. Esther couldn't understand why He had said these things, but she didn't care as long as her son knew he was loved and more than that, he was wanted.

> I AM NOT ASHAMED TO CONFESS THAT I LOVE
> TO BE OF SERVICE
> TO THOSE WHO NEED A WOMAN'S HELP.
> AND WHENEVER THE NEED ARISES
> - ON WHATEVER DISTANT SHORE -
> I ASK NO GREATER OR HIGHER PRIVILEGE
> THAN TO MINISTER TO IT.
>
> MARY SEACOLE

Final Campaign

> Divorce Fair by the Orion Group London Thursday 20th February 2020
>
> The major Divorce Fair is coming to London! We are bringing all specialists and experts you need into one place to help you thrive.

Esther had seen the event pop up on her Instagram account several times, and each time she had an overwhelming urge to attend, unsure if it was curiosity or to seek help. She booked it on Eventbrite and arranged for childcare.

She arrived early enough to browse the stalls, stopping at each stall to talk and gain information. She was right to attend, each company and service stall, was indeed there to help anyone wishing to thrive, after a separation or divorce. She spoke to Solicitors, Families need Fathers, Mediations services, Empower Me Coaches, Yoga /Pilates coaches, Dad.info, Co-parenting organisations (2houses.com), Dating Coaches, Divorce Coach Specialist, all manner of resources to cater for one's wellbeing, all in one venue.

Esther sat and listened to speakers from each of the stalls presenting information about their individual services. There was everything she needed to help her move on. Esther had always attended courses, before Him, she loved to learn and keep up to date with new changes in legislation. He would be in agreement at the beginning of their relationship but over the years when the time arrived for her to attend, He would remind her He wasn't able to take time off work, couldn't she ask her mum or it was just inconvenient with His work rota. Over the years Esther would resort to reading as much as she could to keep up to date. She ended up attending fewer courses if any.

Esther attended this conference to seek advice and learn her rights meant she could now plan what to do. She was more than ready to move on; she had stopped caring about Him, even when they were together.

His treatment of the children only cemented her longing to complete the final stage of her exit from this situation. Her mind-set was different, and being at the Divorce Fair that day helped her now to want to thrive after her divorce. She travelled home with a plan and a purpose. Sitting on the bus going home, Esther sat reflecting and lost in her thoughts.

Life is like a journey, watching scenery whizzing pass,
Whim or fancy, we can stay on or dance last.

Arriving looking lavish or bare, depending on their charm,
Some can divert or lure us from our path,
With us unknowingly falling for their craft.

Inviting us to take another route and messing up our past
We think this is our purpose and think is our last chance.
The moments of great joy with moments of great gasps.

Depending on the driver, who guides us on this route,
Them tightly holding their grasp, we fall under their deception and their grasp.

For all who have strayed from their chosen paths,
please be reminded you will always have another chance.

Elaine Duffus

Esther knew He would try to find a way to draw her back into the battlefield, but now she wanted out of this war, off this racing car that was heading one-way, self-destruction. Esther had her own plans. She and her children were coming off this rollercoaster.

> The impact of Covid-19 on women and children experiencing domestic abuse and the lifesaving services that support them.
>
> We know that government advice on self or household isolation will have a direct impact on women and children experiencing domestic abuse. Home is not likely to be a safe place for survivors of domestic abuse. We are concerned that social distancing and self-isolation will be used as a tool for coercive and controlling behaviour by perpetrators and will shut down routes to safety and support.
>
> Source: www.Womensaid.org.uk
> Until women and children are safe.

Esther watched as the world Covid-19 pandemic slowly unrolled from country to country.

Esther's friend had confided to her their ex-partner was using the pandemic not to see his child and to reduce the maintenance, as He had alleged self-isolated, furlough and working from home. However, she had found out; otherwise, anything to avoid responsibility for his child.

On hearing this, Esther felt she would not be exempt from His usual assault during this period. He would be unable to complete His usual military assault on her, contact times, so would have to find a way to release His anger on her. Esther emailed her barrister for advice. Their son may remain at home, if there was a lockdown, due to their son's underlying medical condition. Esther waited as she always did.

> Marrying and divorcing a narcissist is rough but co-parenting with a narcissist is almost impossible. The demands, attacks, threats, and attempts to inflict guilt are skilful, they rattle a parent, sabotaging his or her mental health.
>
> However, awareness of the narcissist dysfunctional factors protects the parent struggling in this situation. Once these relational patterns are identified, it is easier to co-parent with a narcissist.
>
> Source: Co-parenting with a Narcissist. Section of the article written by Erin Leonard Ph. D Peaceful Parenting posted Jul 08.2018.

His email arrived a week later. It began well, stating the obvious situation of the UK, Covid 19 pandemic and that it would not be wise for their youngest son to have contact, ending with the statement *'Make sure you're keeping my son safe.'*

His final sentence just to remind her what to do and His expectations of her.

Esther would have been surprised if He had asked how they were, did they have enough provisions. Even she lived in the hope that with a pandemic everything could be forgotten and there could be some amicable relationship now. But Esther was very worried. This was too easy. He never made positive suggestions for their son to remain at home.

She replied ignoring His snide comment and agreed especially as their youngest son did not wish to be away from his brothers and offered Him WhatsApp video contact, requesting dates and times, so that their son would not miss His calls. As the court order mentioned James, Esther also informed Him that James had also been offered Video contact and would prefer not to.

> To them, communication is not about understanding. It's a win-lose game. They use verbal abuse and/or violence to accomplish this. They are frequently self-centred, impatient, unreasonable, insensitive, unforgiving, lack empathy and are often jealous, suspicious, and withholding. Their moods can shift from fun-loving and romantic to sullen and angry. Some punish with anger, others with silence or both, It's often 'their way or the highway.'
>
> Source: Do's and Don'ts in confronting abuse
> by Darlene Lancer, LMFT.

When Esther opened His email reply expecting WhatsApp video contact details, when she observed He had addressed her by her maiden name only, she knew this was going to be unpleasant. His reply was lengthy; she knew He had sort assistance with this. His usual replies were only a couple of lines, at the most;

The 1st paragraph outlining that this is not shared care and He had sought legal advice, as advised by her. Why was she cancelling contact? He outlined the contact times in the order. She should welcome having respite from the children.

The 2nd paragraph pointed out to her that they were their children and not hers, offering her Skype to see how their sons were doing once he had them in His contact time.

3rd paragraph outlined that if she called the police, He would ask them to enforce the order, which He assured her they would do.

Final paragraph said that she should stop swearing at Him, as this was not the language He or the children used. Any evidence of harassment would be coming from her.

It ended with Him asking her to send the pickup details, give His children His love and 4 kisses.

PS - Attached was a link. When Esther opened it, this outlined amicable contact arrangements during Covid 19. Esther went back and checked her reply email. There was no denying contact, no harassment mentioned and definitely, no swear words. How she wished she had not responded.

Then she went into protective parent mode, calling everyone, barristers, and police. The youngest son did not want to leave his brothers; he was scared as when he attended the last contact; there was a family member who was very unwell. With Covid 19, their son did not want to be around anyone who was unwell and was scared. The advice was clear if she felt their son was to stay at home, then she was to do this, in their son's best interest.

Esther explained if his father came, she might have to go by the court order, their son began to cry, uncontrollably, he didn't want to go. Esther reassured him she would find a way, she couldn't afford for him to have an asthma attack now, the thought of attending a hospital frightened her. Her younger son was now calmly lay on his bed, staring at the ceiling, she could see the worry on his face. Esther had a flashback to when James was told he had to attend contact and his uncontrollable reactions. She could not allow her younger son to react this way. Esther would have to find another solution even though she wasn't sure what to do.

Esther sent Him another email outlining the government guidelines and that He would not be able to take their youngest son to His elderly parents, where contact takes place, He would also be placing His parents at risk.

He sent just another government link telling her to read paragraph in sec. 1. Esther didn't bother to read it and sent another email. Their youngest son's health comes first, and he is to remain at home with his brothers and not to go to his elderly grandparents, as this was not safe for His parents' wellbeing.

His email now stated He was putting His son's health first reminding her that she had stated no further contact but for good. Also, finally reminding her that children can move between homes, with separated parents.

Esther felt His shift and moved to offer Skype/WhatsApp and that their youngest son was not leaving the house in a pandemic.

His final email accused Esther of using COV-19 to block His contact. The contact He initially cancelled several emails before. He then informed her He would not listen to her lies anymore. Esther was now lost in a sea of emotions, and then she got it. This was not about contact with the children. He wanted to go into battle, frighten her, and more importantly abuse her. The contact had stopped, and He had no way to reach her other than emails.

Esther's friends had told her that her ex-partner had reduced payments to their children using Covid-19 as the reason for the reduced payments. Esther received His full contribution including the correct arrears, including instalment payments. Esther felt something was coming. He had never in 5 years ever paid His full contribution to the children. They sent their schedule, and He would reduce the payments, especially the arrears to the lowest amount to pay back, £5.00 per month on top of the agreed amount.

Esther's instincts had never failed her.

A Very Civil Matter - Elaine Duffus

> **Tech abuse**
> Domestic violence takes lives and ruins lives., affecting one woman in four at some point in her life in England and Wales alone, and killing two women every week. Modern technology gives perpetrators ever-growing ways to stalk, isolate and control women using everyday tools of modern life.
>
> We have found a rise in the number of women whose children's iPads, Xboxes and PlayStations have been hacked by perpetrators to gain access to their accounts, to trace information such as the child's location, who they were speaking to and what games they play.
>
> Source: Tech Abuse Refuge.org.uk

Esther had given her youngest son a phone for his birthday, earlier that year. Their son wanted to take it to his father, and she was reluctant but agreed after all what harm could it do. Esther asked their son to add His number and their son had looked at her asking why? He just needed to take his phone to call her. Esther agreed. He now knew their son had a phone and added His details. He had even sent her a few messages, using their son's phone, asking where she was going? She knew it wasn't her son. Their son would never speak to her in this manner. Once her youngest son had returned home, he confirmed it was his father that had sent the messages over to her and had asked him to unlock the phone to add His details.

Esther felt an uneasiness as this would re-establish a way to send her messages, using His WhatsApp profile to convey them, but with Covid ! 9 she had to allow the contact to remain by this mobile.

Esther was spot-on correct, and It began with a teddy bear with the message written *'I am blessed'*; then He moved it to flash cars. When He loaded a profile picture of a man showing his muscles, the boys became fearful and blocked His number. Esther unblocked the mobile, each time she realised what the boys had done. They did not want her threatened. Esther explained to them it was His phone, and he could display any picture he wanted. Their youngest son had explained. His father did not have WhatsApp before until He saw their youngest son had a phone with WhatsApp.

Esther remembered the pictures He had placed on His WhatsApp profile for her to view, many years ago, the courts were not amused with His actions; hence their only communication was by email. He was using their son's WhatsApp to send her messages. She emailed Him that the boys felt His last WhatsApp profile was a threat to her. The picture remained the same. Esther decided to take her own advice and ignore all negativity and reminded the boys also to do so.

The isolation had Esther now realising that they needed to sort out the last remaining financial connection with Him and felt this was the best time to cut all ties with Him. *'Mum he's changed His profile to this.'* Her youngest son sent over a picture of a sports car. Well, now she knew what He would spend His finance on. She checked her Instagram, having this sinking feeling, and she was right. He had just newly set up his Instagram, with the identical sports car and was trying to follow her. She blocked Him from her Instagram account.

> The term "Intimate partner violence" (IPV) describes physical violence, sexual violence, stalking and psychological aggression (including coercive acts) by a current or former intimate. An intimate partner is a person with whom one has a close personal relationship that can be characterized by the following: Emotional connectedness.
> Source: Definition |Intimate Partner Violence | violence www.cdc.gov/violnceprevention/intimatepartnerviolence

He would end His telephone calls telling their youngest son. He had to go now because He had to go out and save lives.

Thursday night they were clapping for specific Keyworkers, Esther and the boys remaining inside quietly, listening to the outside world clap and drum. On NHS and carers days everything came out, pots and pans drumming in unison with the nation in appreciation. Esther wondered would they the public clap if they knew that some of their key workers were going home and sending specific emails of abuse, would they clap then?

> **Being single and happy
> is better than being sad
> and afraid in an abusive relationship**
>
> Abusive and Toxic Relationship Quote

Isolation is the best time to think and make life changes for the best plans of your life, Esther thought. The isolation had made her feel safer, a respite season. She wanted to leave this lockdown with having nothing attached to Him, and at least to start some processes.

The next battle would be her final. The children were now coming to the age to decide for themselves, especially if they had contact. Esther had always planned to wait, at least until their youngest son went into secondary school to resolve matters. However, she felt to wait was to waste more time on Him. She didn't want to waste time or energy. She wanted to live her best life. Esther wrote to him directly to look at all their options and come to some amicable agreement.

Apart from the sports cars pictures, His other response was to employ a solicitor who wrote to her as if she was nothing, threatening to freeze her assets and questioning her character. Esther thought this was a joke, so decided to speak directly to His solicitor. She wanted to minimize fussing and fighting. She realised this was no joke, but He was now planning to take her to court as soon as possible. His solicitor began each email politely and then as she read on, it became more and more belittling. He had chosen His solicitor well, and if this were a couple of years or even weeks ago, Esther would have crumbled, but she had what she needed now knowledge.

It was their son's birthday and they planned to stay up to just after 12 midnight to say Happy Birthday and then go to bed. This tradition never lost its thrill.

Esther woke to her younger son sending her over the WhatsApp profile picture He had now displaying. This was more adult with a man and a woman. Her son was distressed and wanted to block Him. Esther explained this was His phone, and He could display what he wanted. She decided to take her own advice and ignore Him. He expected her to respond.

Esther had sent His solicitor a further email, on Sunday evening, it was the only time she could use the one laptop they had, Home schooling would begin tomorrow. She expected to receive a reply Monday and to enjoy the rest of the indoor birthday celebrations.

She woke early Monday morning to join her online prayer group, checked her emails and began getting the boys up for Home schooling. Esther opened the email from His solicitor and knew another battle had begun, the words she was reading stunned her – her alleged conduct, client's emotional wellbeing, her apparent on-going manipulative conduct on her part, cruel, manipulative – these words left Esther reeling. He had found a willing educated associate in His combat. She had hoped that this matter would have been resolved with respect, dignity and brought to a mutually satisfactory conclusion.

Esther sighed as she looked at her son, who was now 10; she had spent a little shy of 9 years in court with Him; this was practically all his life. Her older children had enjoyed the luxuries of holidays, birthday treats, toys, not seeing their mother distressed at the arrival of another court date. Esther couldn't afford to give their younger son those things, with everything being eaten up in court fees, finding even paying for essential items a struggle. Esther reflected on the man she had met at Separated Parenting classes and his sadness for his children. Esther now understood that his sadness and her overwhelming sorrow was exactly the same.

The death of an innocent man, George Floyd, impacted on a global level which saw Black people on a whole unite and address the ongoing injustice perpetrated on them as a people.

Esther was not left behind. She had always been aware of, and experienced, racism from school, work, socially, as a wife, as a parent, aunty, daughter – being a black child and then a woman - that teacher who gave her a low grade or didn't think she could achieve a standard of work, 'you must have copied it from a book,' or the teacher you meet years later who thought you must have had 4-5 children by now, at aged 20, and was surprised you had no children. All this even though, Esther wore skirts down to her ankles and jumpers that reached up to her neck, her conservative way of dressing remained.

Entering into the workplace made the injustice come to the forefront, being allocated making hot drinks even though she was qualified in business. Entering a family, as a wife, who thought they were better than her, then defending her sons from nursery to college and beyond, each of her Black son having different battles, Esther had to defend, from bullying from peers to bullying from teachers. Esther watched Michael Holding, Cricket Commentator and former Cricketer, give a powerful message leaving no stone unturned, speaking painfully and with tears in his eyes, of his personal heartache from his own father not being accepted by his mother's family because he was of a darker skin tone. Esther cried with him.

But nothing had prepared Esther to the awakening she felt from Him. He had geared everything, to place her at the ultimate disadvantage – noting her down as a Black Jamaican woman in the court system - the women who some people wanted to imitate their walk, talk and dress sense but not to the point of living their life. A Jamaican woman was seen as aggressive, loud and uneducated, so far from beautiful.
He knew the system from the inside and their dislike of the Black community, especially how the Black woman was seen, would stand in His favour and conceal His attacks. It was the ultimate unseen elephant in the room. For Esther, as a Black woman, the ultimate betrayal was that He was one of her own community.

> **Believe Us**
>
> You may not see the bruises or the abrasions
> Believe Us
> You may not see the cuts or fallen teardrops
> Believe Us
> You may not see the black eyes or painful hurt
> Believe Us
> You may not be present at the beatings or the cursing
> Believe Us
> You may not see the broken bones or busted lips
> Believe Us.
> For Goodness, sake Believe Us.
>
> For all the women that are never believed.
>
> Elaine Duffus 1st June 2020

Esther knew the battle was not over physically, but in her mind, she was free.

How Esther conducted herself in this battle would determine how long she stayed in it.

Esther listened to the song a version sung by Ms Shelby J - 'You got a friend' - and the words 'And all storms run out of rain.' She knew she was never alone.

This Woman
Has Fought A Thousand Battles
And Is Still Standing
Has Cried A Thousand Tears
And Is Still Smiling
Has Been Broken
Betrayed
Abandoned
Rejected
But She still Walks Proud
Laughs Loud
Lives Without Fear
This Woman is Beautiful
This Woman Is Humble
This Woman Is Me!

Thank you for reading this book.
If you need help or support below is a list of resources you may access;

Refuge
For women and children.
Against domestic violence.

The National Domestic Abuse
Helpline is confidential and available
24 hours a day
0808 2000 247
www.refuge.org.uk

women's aid
until women & children are safe

www.womemsaid.org.uk
Opening Hours
Monday – Friday - 10.00am-4.00pm
Saturday and Sunday 10.00am-12.00pm

A list of Resources to empower your journey after you leave and aid in your journey:

Pam Shergill, Director and Personal Life Coach
Empowering Coaching Ltd,
pam@empoweringmecoaching.co.uk
+449(0) 788 188 390

Corrina Bordoli, Co-founder Director
Toddler Tunez creative babysitting
rector
managementtoddlertunez.com
www.toddlertunez.com
07518 592955

Gill Ruidant Founder & CEO
2houses.com Family communication facilitator
gil@2houses.com
=32 (0)71 810 3060

Divorce Goddess Podcast
@divorce goddess
@ tosbrittan

Meet The Author

Elaine Duffus is a poet, writer and author of her first book, A Very Civil Matter.

Born in London, she is the youngest of a blended family.

Her studies and professional background began in the Business sector but her passion to encourage and motivate others, saw her move into the Health and Social Care sector.

She began as a Residential Social Worker and moved onto becoming a Deputy Manager, in an Inner London Children's Residential Home. There Elaine discovered her passion for teaching and training others in this field, moving on to becoming a Freelance NVQ Assessor, working with Community professionals - foster carers, youth workers, mental health staff, nurseries staff and a range of professionals in schools. She is also an accredited Preparing to Teach in the Lifelong Learning Sector (PTLLS) Trainer.

Elaine enjoys attending church and will always be found involved in Children's Ministry and Hospitality Ministry and has had the honour of making several trips, as the Co-Ordinator of an Orphanage Care Programme in Zimbabwe, raising much-needed funds for Orphan, who have lost their families through HIV/AIDS, to cover their educational and equipment costs.

Elaine is able to shine as she uses her innate skills and talents to help colleagues.

Elaine is a mother to 3 sons and loves to teach and inspire and derives tremendous satisfaction by tutoring within the local community, especially children with additional needs.

Her life experience gives her a unique voice to speak to matters around the topic of abuse and /or domestic violence, and it is her deepest wish to be a source of encouragement to all who encounter such instances.

In the words of Bishop Windsor Queensborough *'I am not an expert; however, I want to be a signpost to direct others to the necessary help they need.'*

She also loves to travel, going to the theatre, reading, all the while enjoying 'making memories' with her family.

Lightning Source UK Ltd.
Milton Keynes UK
UKHW020207050621
384939UK00005B/112/J